POSTS TO PROFIT$

POSTS TO PROFIT$

The social media marketing blueprint for building a profitable six-figure online business

Simon J Mitchell

Maverick Goose Ltd

Published by:

Maverick Goose Ltd; https://www.maverickgoose.co/

Posts to Profits: The social media marketing blueprint for building a profitable six-figure online business

By Simon Mitchell

Tradepaper ISBN: 978-1-3999-6176-9

EBook ISBN: 978-1-3999-6231-5

Cover design by Simon Mitchell

Illustrations: Simon Mitchell

Edited by Simon Mitchell

This book is for all those who thought I would fail. Thank you for the fire. It was a pleasure to burn your doubt to the ground.

CONTENTS

FOREWORD IX

INTRODUCTION XIII

1. WHAT IS THE POST$ TO PROFIT$ PROCESS? 1

2. THE GRAVITY METHOD 5

3. YOUR PEOPLE 13

4. YOUR WORLD 33

5. VISION 39

6. VALUES 47

7. VOICE 57

8. VISUALS 65

9. VEND 73

AN INTERLUDE... 115

10. YOUR GRAVITY 119

11. THE 6-STAGE CONTENT STRATEGY 125

12. STAGE 1: PLAN 135

13. STAGE 2: CREATE 153

14. STAGE 3: POST 177

15. STAGE 4: INTERACT 183

16. STAGE 5: GENERATE 195

17. STAGE 6: SELL 255

18. THE 10 SOCIAL MEDIA COMMANDMENTS 269

19. THIS IS NOT YOUR MOTIVATIONAL SPEECH 281

20. ACKNOWLEDGEMENTS 287

21. THE END 293

FOREWORD

By Dan Meredith

When Simon asked me to write the foreword for this book, I was genuinely honoured for two reasons. First, in today's rather ridiculous online world, people need this book. Second, I've seen Simon's concepts go from ideas to success for himself and hundreds of clients. He's changed their lives and businesses in the process.

Simon's marketing approach is very much aligned with my own. It's based on tried-and-tested principles that have 'time-served'. In *Posts to Profits*, Simon has brought these concepts crashing into the social media age.

Should you read and apply this book?

Well, it depends.

This might not be the ringing endorsement you want to hear, but Simon will likely agree. If you're someone who is:

...looking for a quick fix

...not prepared to try new things and challenge existing beliefs.

...unable to grasp that success (yes, even online) takes a) time, b) effort, and c) the tenacity and resilience to keep going.

...then it's not for you. But if you're the opposite of that...

If you picked up this book because you want a better life for yourself—to be your own boss.

If you want to harness the power of social media to build a personal brand.

If you want to make a great living from what you carry around in your pocket every day. (Yes, you can run a successful business with a mobile phone. I do, as do many others).

So, if that's you?

Read the book.

Do what Simon says (I had to get that in...) for time.

Post.

And eventually?

Profit.

I know Simon personally and how good he was as a fitness professional, podcaster, and now marketer. What made him good at these things allowed him to test, tweak, try, fail, try again, and optimise over and over again.

He is a GEEK!

He loves finding out a) what works and b) how to make what works work for him and his clients. I've spent almost 3 years watching Simon do this, and quite frankly, it would have bored me to tears to do it for that long. So, after coaching him all those years ago, I paid him to teach me all his "secrets." Ha!

Simon's distilled years of knowledge and his unique process into this book. If you apply what you learn, it should work out well for you.

I take writing book intros and giving recommendations seriously. I've built a 7-figure business from scratch and sold over 1 million copies of my book *How To Be F*cking Awesome*. After spending ten years in the online space, I know that your reputation matters. This is why I am more than happy to write this foreword. You, Dear Reader, are in Simon's safe (albeit Lego-obsessed) hands.

No gimmicks. No flashy nonsense. No selling your soul to the social media Gods... Just 100+-year-old marketing principles brought up to speed for the social media age.

So get reading, get applying, get posting and get those profits. You and your business deserve it.

I'll close with this:

There's never been a better time to create a business you love with genuine financial freedom. Is it going to be easy? No. But with the right help, you could live a wildly different life—a life better than you ever thought possible.

The best time to start?

The past.

The next best time?

NOW.

So get posting ;-)

Dan Meredith

INTRODUCTION

There comes a time when the elastic snaps. When you push yourself to breaking point, and everything crashes down. My breaking point came on a gloomy Monday morning commute in 2015. Sitting in my car, waiting for the lights to change, I looked at two guys in their cars on either side of me. They looked as miserable as I felt. At that moment, I burst into tears. *"What the fuck was I doing with my life?"* I was unhappy in my personal life and hated my job. I couldn't see a way out. I was too invested in my career; too old to start again.

Looking back, I didn't know jack shit about building a fitness business. Corporate marketing is one thing. Doing everything from scratch alone in a different industry is another. I didn't have a creative agency or a multimillion-pound budget. All I had was a Personal Trainer certificate and the ironparadisefitness.com domain name. Nevertheless, I started building my online empire. Or, as I now refer to it, pissing in the wind for two years.

I would write lousy articles, post selfies, and wonder why clients weren't beating down my virtual door. Desperate to carve a way out of corporate life, I vowed not to quit. My business was my obsession. Going out, meeting friends, and taking a break were a rarity. I thought it was the only way to be successful. I became a hermit. A recluse. Like the creepy guy kids fear in horror movies.

"That's Old Man Mitchell from No. 29. He never leaves the house."

"Some say he only goes outside to dispose of the dead bodies."

I wasn't that bad, but my social life went on ice. I studied nutrition and learned the intricacies of exercise mechanics. I read books and invested in courses on social media, copywriting, and web design. Iron Paradise Fitness had consumed my entire life, and I loved it. It was the fire in my belly I'd been missing. The passion I needed. Although, it did make for awkward conversations on Tinder dates.

"What do you like to do in your spare time?" The innocent question would come.

"Well, I'm building my own business right now, so that's my main focus."

"Ah, cool. But what do you like to do for fun?"

"Work on my business."

"Yeah, but what about when you're not doing that?"

"I'm either working on my business, thinking about working on my business, or eating."

"Oh!..."

I was a lousy first date, but I didn't care. Building my business was everything. Earning money from a business I had built from nothing is indescribable. But I had a problem. A huge problem.

Despite all my efforts, growth was slow. I thought I could scale the business to match my current income and then make a simple switch. It wasn't going to plan. Ultimately, I realised I would never earn a full-time wage with part-time effort. I had to go all in but lacked the courage to leap into the unknown. That was until a random conversation on Friday, February 23rd, 2018.

I remember it like it was yesterday. A guy who worked for me told me how many years he had left before retirement. In a moment of quiet contemplation, I realised I had thirty years left. Thirty years in this open-plan human chicken coop! Thirty years of meaningless presentations and worrying if I was using the corporate-approved font. Thirty years of dumb spreadsheets and watching senior managers puff their chests in pointless meetings. No, thanks. It was now or never. I was single; no kids. The only person's life I would mess up would be mine. I arrived in the office the following Monday with fear in my soul and doubt in my bones. I quit. In the late spring of 2018, with a side hustle that made almost no money, I kissed goodbye to job security, a luxury car, and an £80,000 salary. I had had enough.

The game was on. Iron Paradise Fitness was generating £900 a month. Not enough to pay the bills and put food on the table, let alone rent a Lamborghini and waft a fake Rolex Daytona on Instagram. I had enough savings to keep me afloat for six months. After that, I would be out of cash and pleading for my old job. Some said I was crazy. Others told me I'd be back, begging bowl in hand. This was all the "fuck you fire" I needed. If I failed, it wouldn't be because I didn't give it everything. So, I turned to what I knew best; marketing. I applied every ounce of marketing knowledge to my fitness business. Five years and two successful businesses later, I'm still here. I still don't own a begging bowl.

Don't get me wrong. It wasn't easy. Surviving the first two anxiety-filled years was a minor miracle. Self-doubt engulfed me at the dawn of every new month. What if all my clients simultaneously quit? What if I couldn't get any leads? I'm not cut out to be a coach. I was delusional to think I could run a business.

In late-2019, I almost closed the doors for good. I invested over £3,000 in an agency that promised me leads on tap from Facebook ads. The return on my investment? About £150. Rather than leads on tap, the pipes were blocked, and I was leaking money. But the lousy advice didn't stop there. I paid one business mentor almost £2,000 for 12 weeks of coaching. After two weeks of radio silence, I chased him to see what was happening. *"Glad you called, Simon. I've been working on your strategy. Are you free this Friday for me to talk you through it?"* Call me cynical, but I didn't believe a word he said. Regardless, I jumped on a video call later in the week to hear his wise words. This is the paraphrased version of the conversation.

"I want you to search for Facebook Groups that your ideal clients might use." He said.

"Ok. Then what?" I replied.

"Start following as many people as possible." He said with an eagerness in his voice. It was as if he'd cracked the secret social media marketing code.

"Ok. Then what?" I replied. Still unsure about where this was heading.

"That's it. People will see your follow request, look at your profile, and start messaging you." He said.

"That's not how this works, and I'm not doing that. Think of something else." I said, in a blunt, I-can't-believe-what-you've-just-said tone. Safe to say, our coaching relationship didn't survive a third week

I ditched the business mentors spouting hyperbole and went back to the basic principles of marketing. Two months after almost hitting rock bottom, things started to change. My podcast exploded and hit No. 7 in the UK and US fitness charts, eventually growing to over one million downloads a year. My Instagram grew consistently, along with my authority in the industry. I started getting consistent leads without much effort. Not only that, but I was converting leads to high-end coaching programmes via email. No sales call required.

I used the same principles when I launched my social media marketing business, Maverick Goose Ltd, in 2021. My first product launch generated over £20k in revenue within its first month. The subsequent three launches also exceeded 5 figures in their first month, with another breaking £20k. In the first six months of trading, I'd blasted through $100k in revenue. All organic. Zero paid advertising. The process I followed revealed something astonishing, though not exactly ground-breaking. You can build a thriving online business by delivering excellent service and following basic marketing principles. And it's these marketing principles that you'll discover in this book.

Bad marketing advice is like a venereal disease spreading through a Magaluf holiday resort. It's unstoppable. Most business coaches were simply in the right place at the right time. They capitalised on the novelty of social media, gained notoriety, and monetised their sizeable following. Those days are over. What worked for them won't work for you. Don't expect to build your online business using their out-of-date hacks. These tactics work long enough for the coach to cherry-pick a few testimonials. But when the honeymoon period is over, where does that leave you? Confused and constantly flipping from one tactic to the next.

I often speak to business owners who post great content — it's valuable and looks professional — but they struggle to get more than a handful of likes, let alone leads or sales. These coaches spend hours on social media because they think it's what they're supposed to do, yet they have to fight like stink for every client. It's getting harder to grow a following on social media with each passing year. Competition is growing, and every market feels saturated. It's difficult to stand out from the crowd. It feels impossible to reach your target audience amongst the social media noise. The harsh truth is that the competition will leave you behind if you don't solve the problem soon. By the time you figure it out, social media will have moved on, and you'll be back to square one; again. This brings me to why I am writing this book.

Entrepreneurs are failing. Online businesses are dying. Beaten to death by bad advice and choked from the inside by a lack of confidence. As someone who almost failed, I want to give you a proven pathway and the right strategy to turn posts into profits.

I had doubts about publishing this book. After all, I'm not a billionaire. I'm not even a millionaire. I haven't scaled to seven figures, bought a luxury yacht, and dominated the stock market. What right do I have to teach you about social media marketing?

After reading hundreds of business books, I can count on one hand the ones that directly impacted my business. Most were the lofty musings of the super-rich. Few contained tangible strategies. I wanted to read books written by successful entrepreneurs *while* they were growing. I wanted to hear the stories of struggle, success, and self-doubt as they happened. I wanted to know that it wasn't me, that it was part of the process. This is that book. This is me on the way up. How far I'll get, I have no idea. But I hope that by sharing everything I know, I'll bring you along for the ride.

P.S. I've compiled exclusive bonus resources to accompany the book. Only readers of this book can access these bonuses. To get your hands on them, go to poststoprofitsbook.com

Chapter 1

WHAT IS THE POST$ TO PROFIT$ PROCESS?

"I'm pretty much fucked."

Entrepreneurs, when they realise building an online business is 95% marketing

Entrepreneurs with online service businesses want to solve problems. Copywriters want to help their clients sell more stuff. Fitness, nutrition, and life coaches want to transform people's lives. Business coaches want to guide people to six-and-seven-figure incomes. Vocal coaches want to teach the next global superstar how to reach their full potential. Therapists want to heal people's trauma. None of them wants to build complex websites, sales pages, and opt-in automation. None of them wants to edit videos and create beautiful graphics worthy of display in The Louvre. None of them wants to waste hours online sending cold DMs and fending off trolls. But it's the crushing reality for many who dream of living the freedom lifestyle. There's no avoiding it. You must learn how to market your business to have any hope of making money. And, unless you're working in marketing, you'll have to learn new skills. Fast!

Posting content and building a massive following is the shortcut to success (or so the story goes). But the bright lights of social media leave would-be entrepreneurs blinded to reality. Struggling entrepreneurs fuss over likes and followers, trapping themselves in "engagement anxiety." The glaring problem—no marketing strategy—stays unresolved. Instead, getting more engagement remains the only goal. It's madness. But this is the distorted view of marketing in a world where social media status is king.

But social media marketing doesn't have to be a frustrating, never-ending learning curve. There is an easier way—a way to spend less time flooding social media with content and "giving value." A way to focus on what you do best and avoid the lead-less Lemmings walking straight off the marketing cliff. The way is, of course, The Posts to Profits process.

My aim is not to make you the world's greatest marketer. My goal is to give you just enough information to generate the largest returns and then let you move on with life. Think of the following 250 pages as a sojourn—a temporary stay in the marketing world. Once you have what you need, feel free to leave and only return when you need guidance. This doesn't mean it'll be a cinch, or you'll get the skills overnight. Heck! You'll need to do more than read this book to master the marketing basics. You have to take what you learn and put it into practice. Because it's not about how many books you read, boxes you tick, or even how you fill your time. It's how these activities change you and your business. So, there's hard work ahead. But, if you're up for it, the Posts to Profits process will make it easier than ever. But if the thought of hard work is disappointing news, stop reading. Close the book and move on to some manifestation clap-trap.

This Posts to Profits process won't work miracles. But it will give you a rock-solid social media marketing strategy. You'll learn the techniques to attract your ideal prospects and convert them into clients. No massive following required. No soul-sucking trends. And no spam tactics and cold DMs.

The Posts to Profits process comprises six stages.

- Assess the gaps
- Define your strategy
- Get leads
- Make sales
- Consistency
- Mastery

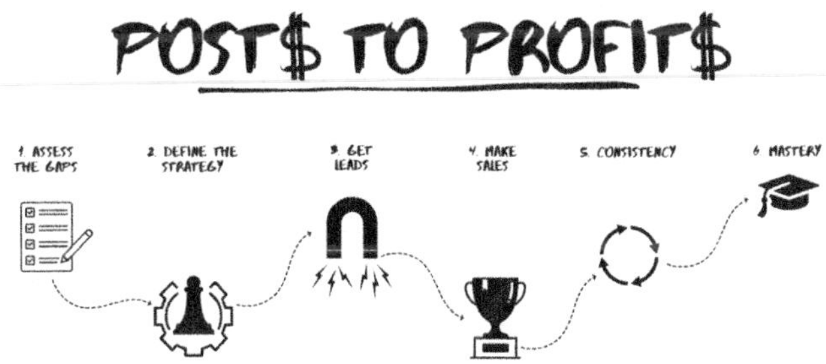

It's difficult to assess the gaps in your marketing in a book. Writing a long list of questions would be a literary sedative. So, I've created a free online Content Health Check. You'll find it at poststoprofitsbo ok.com. The assessment helps you understand what you're doing well and what needs attention. Plus, you'll receive a personalised report and suggested next steps for improvement.

While planning this book, it became evident I couldn't cram everything into one volume. I suspected you wouldn't want to read a 1,500-page tome, so the book focuses on strategy, leads, and sales. These elements give you the foundations of a profitable online business. This is far more crucial than worrying about mastering complex marketing strategies. At least for now...

We begin our marketing adventure with The Gravity Method.

Chapter 2

THE GRAVITY METHOD

"You may hate gravity, but gravity doesn't care."
Clayton M. Christensen

Ever feel out of your depth in your business? Like you're in the middle of the Atlantic Ocean, 500 miles off the coast of America, and the sharks are circling. Some call it Imposter Syndrome. I call it being shit-scared of failure. This is how I felt when a high-end gym chain asked me to create its social media strategy in 2019.

I was still a one-man fitness coaching business. I had a background in marketing, and my solo business was growing, but this was different. I was okay with winging it, failing, and figuring everything out on the fly. After all, if things went wrong (which they often did), I could brush it under the carpet and move on. No one would be any the wiser. But taking those risks with someone else's business wasn't an option. I decided to call in reinforcements.

My buddy Rich is a phenomenal sales coach. I figured he'd know a thing or two about pitching for and delivering this sort of work. Rich and I got together and spent two days planning a winning proposal.

The problem was that we didn't understand the business. We needed to see the facility, speak to the team, and see the problems first-hand. The following Friday, Rich and I hopped on a train to London to visit their HQ and meet the manager. On the 90-minute train ride, we discussed our approach to the meeting. We needed a way of communicating our marketing principles and method (which didn't exist as we stepped on the 7:02 to London Euston).

I thought about everything I'd learned in my corporate job and my journey as an entrepreneur. I sketched a crude three-part content marketing ecosystem on a scrap of paper. It wasn't complicated. Audience, Offer, Content. Not exactly ground-breaking. It needed something more—a little pizzazz—to stand any chance of impressing the client. So, I did what any good marketer would do. I dreamt up a catchy name. Audience, Offer, and Content became Your World, Your People, and Your Gravity. The Gravity Method was born.

We didn't win the project. I wasn't mad. I should have turned the opportunity down from the outset. I had no framework, credibility, or business thinking I could help. When the gym owners first asked for support, I was just delusional enough to be totally confident. With every meeting, every video call, every email, I was praying they'd tell us, *"Thanks, but no thanks."* Despite the fortunate failure of our proposal, the Gravity Method stuck in my mind. I began refining my 'back of a fag packet' idea, turning it into a cohesive framework. I added layers of detail to each section, tweaking the formula as I tested new ideas. Niching, positioning, branding, content strategy, building offers. It had everything. In the summer of 2021, I knew I had a process that would help other businesses overcome their social media woes. Two years after its genesis on a train ride to London, I was ready to teach others the Gravity Method.

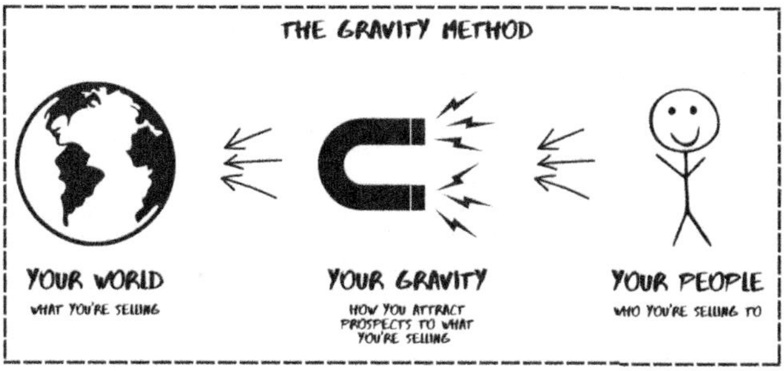

These are the three marketing concepts you need to start getting leads and sales online. Don't let any social media snake oil salespeople tell you otherwise.

I'll put it another way. If you have great products and phenomenal content, but you're communicating to the wrong audience, you won't make sales. If you have amazing products, but your content sucks, the right people won't know you exist, and you won't make sales. And, if you're creating compelling content for the right audience, but they don't want what you're selling, you won't make sales. You must have all three elements of The Gravity Method to start and scale any online business. Resist the temptation of getting distracted by passing trends and useless tactics. Without the fundamentals, any other activity is causing sales to drift further and further away.

I've divided the book into four sections. The first three give you the details behind The Gravity Method, and the fourth helps you bring it all together. For now, here's an overview of The Gravity Method, starting with Your People.

Your people are your ideal customers. The clients you'd love to clone and attract to your business at will. Understanding this perfect customer is crucial. A vague, nebulous niche and attempting to appeal to everyone leads to mediocre sales (at best). It's better to be the go-to person for 1,000 people than the person who 100,000 people forget.

The Gravity Method teaches you the simplest way to find the right niche. The people you'll be passionate about helping and who won't make you dread waking up in the morning. You don't need to know whether your ideal client likes a double-shot vanilla macchiato. You don't need to know their shoe size or favourite breakfast cereal. Unless you're selling macchiatos, trainers, and Frosties, of course. All you need to do is answer one question. I'll tell you what the question is soon.

Entrepreneurs waste an inordinate amount of time and money trying to generate leads. They invest in courses, software, and ads, often overlooking the fundamental issue. An issue that, if left unfixed, throws all businesses into an uncontrollable tailspin. Branding. I don't mean logos, fonts, and colours (although they have their place). Branding is what sets you apart from the competition—your unique identifier. It's the common thread linking your values, offers, and content to your ideal customer. Without a strong brand, you become a commodity, and the only way for customers to assess your worth is through price. Unless you're willing to sell your products at rock-bottom prices, you'll never win that war.

The Gravity Method helps you create a stand-out brand: Your World. It teaches you to think of your business as a planet. Your World's core is your mission: why you do what you do. Layered on top of this are your values, visual branding, products, and services. Create a world designed for your ideal customers, and you're two-thirds of the way to consistent leads.

The final part of the Gravity Method is the easiest (if you've done everything else correctly). But it's what most online businesses struggle with most: creating profitable content. Your Gravity attracts Your People to Your World (and keeps them there). It's your social media content and lead magnets. This compelling content is the mechanism to get your offers in front of the right people. If your offer sucks and you're pitching to the wrong people, the greatest content in the world won't save you. It's why content is the last component of The Gravity Method. Even though your content sucks, be patient. We've got to rewind to square one: Your People.

PART ONE:

THE GRAVITY METHOD

YOUR PEOPLE

WHO YOU'RE SELLING TO

Chapter 3

YOUR PEOPLE

The Gravity Method: Part One

"No niche is too small if it's yours."

Seth Godin

It was sometime around December 2018 when self-doubt tightened its grip and panic set in. I had been recording podcasts for almost two years, but no one was listening. It doesn't take long for fear and loathing to cloud the mind of a paranoid entrepreneur. So, it was surprising I hadn't quit several months before. But there I was, churning out regular episodes to a few hundred people. It seemed pointless. The voice inside me was screaming, *"Holy Jesus! Give up already."* When I look back years later, the problem is obvious.

Switching from corporate marketing to fitness coaching put me on the defensive. There was a self-imposed need to prove myself—to show my knowledge and gain credibility. I thought I had nailed it. In my mind, I was striking the perfect balance between practical advice and scientific theory. Listening back to those old episodes years later, I couldn't have been more wrong. Every podcast was a trudge through audible treacle. Pointless PubMed references on top of turgid research psychobabble.

The only people who knew what I was talking about weren't even listening. Those who did tune in regretted their decision within seconds. It felt like I was broadcasting on dead airwaves. *"Mayday. Mayday. Can anybody hear me?"* Silence. There was only white noise, static, and several one-star reviews.

Fortunes changed after a sales call with a prospective client. She was from somewhere in the United States: Boston? Delaware? Iowa? I don't recall. She loved listening to the podcast purely for my accent (well, it wasn't for the content). Despite being a fan of the show, she had some constructive criticism. She told me that I had a split personality. To her, I was a cross between James Bond and Gary Vaynerchuk on social media but a suit-and-tie-wearing stiff on my podcast. She was right. I wasn't talking about the wrong topics. I wasn't a coach bereft of new thoughts and anything interesting to say. My delivery was all wrong. Rather than create content for those who wanted to listen, I created content to avoid backlash from my peers. In the end, I pleased no one, not even myself.

Early in 2019, I revamped the podcast. Out went the dry science chat. In came a healthy dose of my true personality. The show went from a 30-minute lecture to a 15-minute chat down the pub with your best mate. It had character, style, and practical solutions. It appealed to a time-poor generation who didn't want to listen to a 90-minute waffle (aka, my niche). It was podcasting SAS-style. In. Out. On to the next one. (I have no idea if this is the style of the SAS. It sounded good, so I left it in).

Designing the show for my niche changed everything. Twelve months later, Lean Life Radio exceeded 60,000 monthly downloads. And it didn't stop. The show grew to almost 90,000 downloads a month by the time it ended. Even though I stopped recording episodes in 2021, the podcast still gets 5,000 - 10,000 downloads every month. I'd have a low-effort side hustle if I wanted to sell something to those listeners. My focus is elsewhere, though; anything I had for sale is now free.

Niching not only saved my podcast, but it also saved my business (and my sanity). The show's growth boosted my Instagram traffic and gave me instant credibility. Instead of short bursts of engagement, I had my ideal client's uninterrupted attention. Long-form content helped me build stronger relationships faster. I became the go-to person for a small group of people, which was all I needed for a profitable business.

What is niching?

"Niching is... and that is what I want, okay?" David Brent (if he was writing this book).

Choosing the right market is a make-or-break decision. Get it wrong, and your business is on the slippery slope to failure from the outset. You could have the most incredible product in the world, but you're doomed if you pitch it to the wrong people. Imagine trying to sell the finest 28-day aged Angus steak to vegan restaurants. It won't work. Don't be the business that sells meat to vegans or ice to Eskimos. Be the business that creates the perfect product for a specific demographic.

The often fatal mistake is targeting a broad niche. It's a decision driven by fear. Fear that channelling efforts into a smaller demographic limits sales.

The fledgling copywriter thinks her writing chops are sharper than Lorena Bobbitt's kitchen knife. When she writes, she sells. Why limit potential revenue by focusing on sales pages for Business Coaches? The simple answer is that people want experts.

Imagine you have an original BMW 3 Series E21 from 1980. It's your baby—your pride and joy. Which of the following garages would you trust when it needs repairs or servicing?

"Series 3 Servicing": a family-owned business specialising in maintaining classic Series 3 BMWs. The father-and-son team has been in business for over four decades. What these two don't know about the 3 Series isn't worth knowing.

The alternative is "Anycar Servicing." This garage prides itself on rock-bottom prices and servicing anything. The garage even has *"We fix anything"* writ large across the front of the building. Most of the Anycar Servicing team have never seen a car from the 80s, let alone serviced one.

The decision is simple. The expert wins almost every time and charges more. Here's a copywriting example.

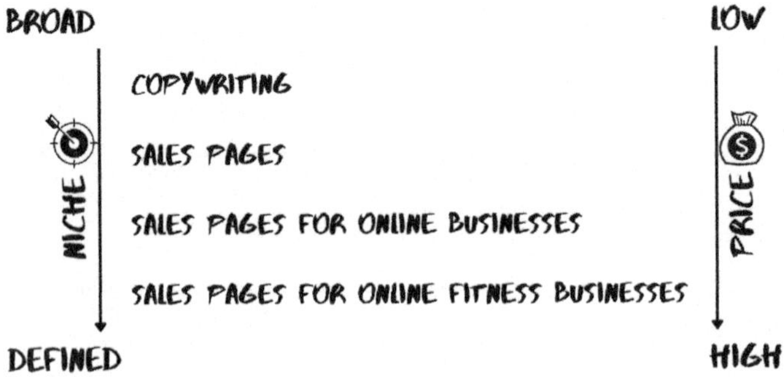

Customers expect to pay for expert knowledge if you offer a specialised service. The more specific the service, the easier it is to market and the more you can charge. Stay too broad, and you rely on attracting customers based on either price, personality, or your gigantic unrivalled reputation (which, I guess, you don't have).

There are situations where staying broad works. In any industry, "unicorn" businesses come along at the right time, with the right product, and hit pay dirt. But, trying to reverse engineer these mythical beasts often leads to failure. So, play the percentages. When your business is in its infancy, niche.

How to choose the right niche

Here's a five-part formula and one key question to help you pick the right niche.

1. Don't choose a market in free fall.

When Netflix started booming, only fools would contemplate opening a Blockbuster-style store. You might have made money while people were considering a move to streaming services. But, the brick-and-mortar rental business was in sharp decline.

A declining market is a ticking time bomb. Soon, you'll run out of selling opportunities and scramble to pivot your business. It's a headache you don't want, so steer clear.

2. They must be easy to find.

Choosing a niche is one thing, but finding them is another. When considering your niche, ask one crucial question. Could I target this audience with an advert? You don't have to start running ads, but if you did, could you target those ads to your niche? If the answer is no, your chances of success, even with organic content, are low.

3. They must have cash

When I was in my early twenties, I was a struggling student. I lived in a dilapidated shared house in Bristol with four random dudes I'd never met. One was a crazy Russian called Ivan, who once smeared his name in blood on a wall in his bedroom. I forget the names of the other three. They didn't leave the same unforgettable impression as Ivan.

One thing this rag-tag bunch of students had in common was a distinct lack of money. Our house was rundown. Every morning, a cornucopia of slugs greeted us in the kitchen. The molluscs slimed in from the garden, climbed the walls and adorned the kitchen surfaces. It was grim. Our nutrition wasn't much better. None of us could cook, so our diets consisted of soup, bread, and super noodles. Any money we did have went on 2-for-1 drinks at the local club on student night.

Like most guys at that age, I wanted to build muscle. My naive mind thought that more muscles equalled more girls—any girls. I had no clue what I was doing. Training consisted of throwing around a set of old dumbbells my Dad gave me. Nutrition wasn't a consideration. I couldn't afford protein, so why bother?

Some fitness coaches might think students like me were the perfect niche. Having been a student themselves, the fresh-faced trainers believe they can empathise; they've been there, too. Eager to launch a booming business, they develop the *90-Day Student Shred programme*. It's £2,000 for the 90-day transformation. It includes everything: training programme, nutrition protocol, supplement recommendations, the lot. The problem is the target market is looking for a solution that's a fraction of the price.

Good luck trying to make sales if your audience can't afford what you're selling. Ensure your product's price matches what your niche expects (and can afford) to pay.

4. You must be able to solve their problems.

The sick buy medicine to cure illnesses. Commuters buy cars for convenience and to become more mobile. Entrepreneurs buy expensive MacBooks to run their businesses from anywhere in the world (and to blend in at hipster coffee shops). These products are solutions to problems. Your product or service must also provide a clear solution. Don't choose a niche because you think it's profitable if you can't help them achieve their desired goal.

5. They must be people with whom you want to do business.

In the early days, you'll work with anyone. Anyone willing to pay you money gets through the door. No questions. No criteria. You don't have much choice. You could be picky about who you work with, but chances are you need the cash. So, prepare yourself for several lousy clients. Think of it as a rite of passage—an initiation every entrepreneur endures. We've all been there. A client once told me they couldn't afford to pay me for two months. Not because they had hit troubled times and money was tight. No, no, no. He defaulted because he bought two jet skis and a pickup truck in a moment of midlife madness.

We all take on clients who make us dread waking up in the morning. Those customers who send whining emails at 2 a.m. to vent about a minor issue that doesn't exist. But don't make it harder for yourself by choosing a niche you have no passion for helping. You'll regret it every day you're in business.

The important question

Who can you help the most? That's it. That's the one crucial question I mentioned earlier. You could complete a complex avatar-defining exercise to pick your niche. My advice? Don't waste your time... yet.

Based on your education, knowledge, skills, experience, and passion, who can you help achieve their goals? Whoever springs to mind is likely a good starting point for defining your niche. Just ensure you consider the first five steps as well.

The 10-minute niche dump

Picking a niche is easy but doesn't automatically lead to more sales. For example, writing *"I help vegans"* on your social media profile won't generate sales. Hordes of prospects won't beat down your virtual door with fistfuls of kale. Understanding a niche inside-out is what makes sales. But it's the task most (unsuccessful) coaches avoid because it's too hard. So let me make it simple.

Grab a piece of paper and a pen. Lock yourself in a room, away from all distractions. Switch off all your devices except your smartphone, which you'll put in aeroplane mode. Next, set a timer for ten minutes. Now write down anything and everything that comes to mind about your chosen niche.

What are their fears, struggles, and mental challenges? What have they tried in the past? How long have they tried to reach their goal, and how does constant failure make them feel? Keep writing. It doesn't have to make sense. Writing disjointed words, phrases, and sentences is okay. The aim is to reach into the depths of your brain and extract every potential information nugget.

Your niche dump often reveals ideas for programme names, sales pages, and content. Don't skip this task. It will help you build the foundations that make content creation a cinch.

Sometimes, this method for choosing a niche doesn't click. People think differently, so it's essential to have alternative options. After all, I don't want you to get stuck at this early stage.

There are two alternative ways to think about your niche. The first is niche by your skills and the specific problems you solve. Think about what you do best. Are you an email automation wizard? Do you write the best sales pages humankind has ever seen? Do you have an uncanny knack for simplifying complex scientific research?

Whatever your zone of genius, you can build your niche around those skills and solving problems. You don't have to niche by demographic.

The second option is to niche by characteristics and psychographics.

Think about aligning with prospects based on their values, fears, goals, and attitudes. Ignore gender, age, and career.

The Problem Path

I can pinpoint the precise moment I cracked the content code. Sitting in my dining room, which doubled as an office at the time, I prepared for a sales call. I spent ten minutes reading through the prospect's pre-call questionnaire. The responses weren't out of the ordinary. The potential client wanted to lose weight, stop yo-yo dieting, and build butt cheeks of steel. Standard fare. But her reply to the final question grabbed my attention.

"Out of all the Cantina bars in all the galaxy, why did you walk into mine?" This was my attempt at humour and a spin on the mundane question, *"Why do you want to work with me?"*

"I binged about 25 episodes of your podcast and read loads of your posts. I loved them all. You answer the questions I've struggled with for ages. It's like you know exactly what I'm thinking."

Hmmm. Interesting.

The sales call lasted five minutes. My content did the selling without me saying a word. The prospect had two choices: hiring me or facing the daunting alternative—going alone. Going it alone meant consuming more content and piecing everything together herself. It would be possible to achieve success, but it's a long, hard road. My content provided the confidence and trust needed for the potential client to commit to coaching.

The question is, How can you do the same? How do you make prospects feel as if you know what they're thinking with alarming accuracy?

Good news! The answer isn't luck, voodoo, or a rare miracle. It's a simple five-step process I call The Problem Path. It's a concept I discovered after reading Alex Hormozi's $100m Offers[1]. Although, he didn't use it for social media or call it the Problem Path. I've tweaked, modified, and adapted the concept for content creation. The Problem Path helps build a content strategy that solves your audience's biggest problems.

First, start by defining your ideal clients' current situation. What are they struggling with? What are their fears and frustrations? What have they tried before? How do they feel about themselves and their chances of success? Ask the questions that make sense for your business. You won't know the answers for certain, so empathise as best you can. (Hint. Your ten-minute niche dump will help).

Next, fast forward 12 months (or whatever time frame you prefer). Your prospect invested in your service, reaped the rewards, and achieved phenomenal results. What does life look like for them now? How do they think, feel, and act? What are they able to do that they couldn't comprehend before?

These are the start and end points of the Problem Path. This gives your content a specific direction.

Lastly, write down all the problems they face getting from A to B. Why can't they do this themselves? Why do they need you? Imagine you're a fitness coach helping people build muscle. Do your ideal clients lack the skills to perform exercises correctly? Are they too busy to plan their food and prepare healthy meals? Have they failed so many times they feel success is impossible? Do they struggle with consistency—always quitting at the first hurdle? List as many problems as possible. The more, the better.

Here's an example an online fitness coach might create if their ideal client is someone who wants to lose weight. This is your ideal client's Problem Path. We'll revisit this in Part Two when we start designing your offer and again in Part Three to create your complete content strategy.

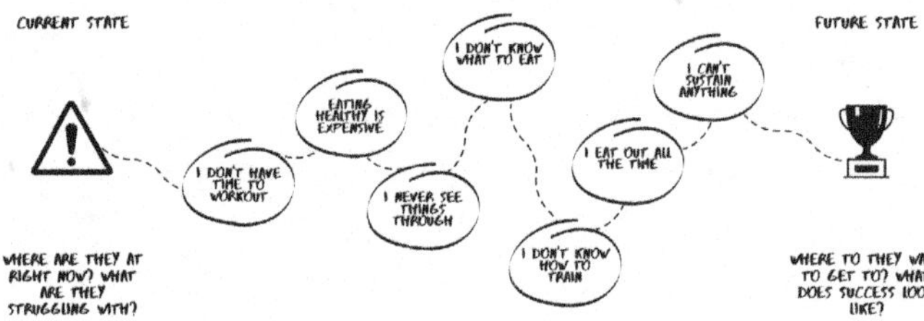

Advanced strategies for understanding your niche

Say the word survey, and you think of random people in hi-viz approaching you in the street asking,

"Can I ask you a quick question?"

"You just did. Have a great day. Bye."

Well, that's the witty retort I wish I had the balls to say. But, the introvert in me crosses the street to avoid all contact.

Reading about surveying your audience might seem dull. But stick with me, my friend. Harness the power of the humble questionnaire, and you can get more email subscribers, more leads, and more sales. Cha-ching!

And there are no clipboards and hi-viz jackets in sight.

This approach to surveying your audience is great whether you're redesigning your service, developing a new lead magnet, or creating a content strategy. It works whenever you need to be sure you're creating something people want. The process works best via email, but I'll cover a social media option, too. Let's start with the survey.

There are myriad software options available. Search online for your preferred option. But don't overthink it. This survey is as basic as it gets, so it doesn't matter what software you use. Heck. Get people to reply to your email with their feedback. Don't get hung up about the technology. On to the questions.

Question 1: The Rating

Start by gauging the potential client's pain. Your service, lead magnet, and content should focus on solving a particular problem, be it weight loss, muscle gain, sales, leads, staff churn, or the lack of mobility in Alaskan Mountain Goats. Define the problem and ask your audience how much they struggle with it. Get them to rate their frustration on a scale of 1-10.

Question 2: Top 3 Struggles

Ask your audience what they struggle with the most. Provide a list of options and ask them to pick three. For example, if the overall problem is weight loss, the multiple-choice list could include,

- Emotional eating.
- Controlling cravings.
- Eating out at restaurants.
- Understanding how much to eat.
- Knowing what to eat.
- When to eat.
- And so on...

This starts to narrow down the problems your audience cares about the most. You can use this data to influence how much content you create about each topic. I'll cover that in Part Three.

Question 3: The Number One Priority

It's time to dig deeper into your audience's motivations. With question three, you define people's number one priority. The one thing that gives them the most pain, stress, and frustration. Provide several options and tell people to pick one. Using the weight loss example above, your list could include,

- Implementing positive habits.
- Adjusting your mindset regarding food and body image.
- Losing weight.
- Learning how to eat whatever you want without guilt.

Question 4: The Format

Get your audience to tell you how they would want to consume the product or service you're about to create. Do they want group coaching, a membership site, an online course, or a simple eBook? You'll never know until you ask.

Provide several options and gauge feedback.

But don't let the answers completely sway you. For example, an eBook might be everyone's first choice, but if you hate writing and can't string a cohesive sentence together, it's a terrible option.

Keep an open mind. Use the feedback to influence, not dictate, your decision.

Question 5: An Open Question

It's important to pose an open question at the end of the survey. This helps your audience become an integral part of the development process. And when your audience feels part of the process, they are far more likely to want (and buy) the final product. Here's an example of a great open question.

> *"What could I include in a free resource or coaching programme that would make it invaluable to you?"*

Responses to this question will also give you plenty of content ideas. Save any responses you get, and use them if you ever get stuck for content.

Question 6: Market Research (optional)

You don't have to include this question, but it could be a great time to find out what has stopped your email subscribers from investing in you. After all, those replying to your survey are your most engaged followers and will give you the best insights. Simply ask, *"Why haven't you invested in [programme name] yet?"* Attach a list of the most common objections: too expensive, I'm working with another coach, etc., and see what people say. Use the feedback to tailor your product or service and guide the copy on your sales pages.

Survey done; what about the email? Well, this is the easy part. You don't need a long email because you're not trying to sell anything. You need a short, punchy email that gets people to complete the questionnaire.

What if you don't have an email list?

What if you have no email list and no email subscribers? How do you survey an audience that doesn't exist? One option is social media. Most social media platforms give you several ways to ask your audience for feedback. You could provide a link to an online survey. You can poll your followers or pose a question, asking people to message you their answers. If you use the latter options, your survey needs a different approach. People are in a different mindset on social media. They're scrolling through content, looking for entertainment and education. The percentage of users who will get excited at the prospect of a six-part online survey is tiny.

Simplify your survey. Ask fewer questions or pose questions over several days. Ask your audience for their Top 3 struggles on day one. Then, follow up a couple of days later, asking about their number one priority.

Surveys on social media are almost always the inferior option. Free text replies lack depth because people are in a rush. Wherever possible, use email or link to third-party software.

"But, Simon. I don't have any social media followers. What do I do?"

"Sounds logical, Simon. But when I survey my audience, no one responds."

If you have no audience, there are still a couple of options before the final resort—guessing. Have you got any previous or current customers that could provide helpful insights? Tap into this existing network even if they're not slap-bang in your target niche.

Don't have any previous clients? Jeez! This is getting tough. Your next option is market research and competitor analysis. Look at what people who have the audience you want are creating. What topics do they often talk about in their content? Do they offer free lead magnets? If so, what problems do they focus on? Build a picture of your ideal client's wants and needs from others servicing that audience.

Still drawing a blank. Well, my friend. You're going to have to guess. Then, refine your approach when you start to build an audience.

PART TWO:

THE GRAVITY METHOD

YOUR WORLD

WHAT YOU'RE SELLING

Chapter 4

YOUR WORLD

The Gravity Method: Part Two

"People buy what you do because you think about why you do it."

Simon Mitchell

Call me gullible. Some years ago—never mind how long precisely—I got sucked into the 'Start With Why' tribe. I watched Simon Sinek's 18-minute TED Talk and any other random clips I could find on YouTube. I bought his book and read it cover to cover twice. Everything started to make sense.

"People don't buy what you do. They buy why you do it."[1] Hallelujah! Praise be! Simon had me believing. The solution to my sales drought was simple. All I needed to do was tell people why I wanted to help them. Armed with the knowledge of my mission—to live the high life in Aruba—clients would sign up in droves.

---

1. Sinek, Simon. (2011). Start With Why: The Inspiring Million-Copy Bestseller That Will Help You Find Your Purpose

Call me Sinek-cal (see what I did there), but 'Start With Why' is nothing more than a nice idea—a social media sound bite. In Sinek's now famous TED Talk, he uses Apple as an example of a company that starts with why. But this is where the 'Start With Why' mantra crumbles.

I'm an Apple addict. I'm typing this manuscript on an iMac. My MacBook Pro is next to me, as is my iPhone 13. I'm even listening to Apple Music with my AirPod Pros. Apple products are my meth. Every time Apple releases a new product, I want it. The question is, why? Why don't I buy a Dell computer? Why not choose Bose earphones? Why do I cream myself over the thought of a Pro Display XDR that costs $5k? It's not because of Apple's 'why.' I don't even know what their 'why' is. According to Sinek, your goal is to do business with people who believe what you believe. I have no idea what Apple believes. The only reason I buy their products is that everything just works, and I like feeling superior in overpriced coffee shops. I have no idea if that's Apple's 'why', but it's why I part with my cash.

We buy products for myriad reasons: convenience, recommendation, experience, and quality. Brand values? Mission statements? They don't even make the long list. To hammer this point home, I asked my wife, Maria, to name brands she uses daily. But not any brand that came to mind. I wanted to know which brands she uses and wouldn't consider any other option.

"Name some brands you use daily. Think make-up, clothes, food, coffee, shopping, and household stuff." I asked.

"Hmmm." Maria pondered her choices. It was like she was visualising every item in every room. *"Lavazza coffee, Amazon, The Pink Stuff, Lancome Monsieur Big Mascara, Miel l'Apiculteur honey."*

"Why do you buy Lavazza coffee?" I asked, eager to see if there was any Sinek-esque logic to Maria's selections.

"Because it's the best Asda has available. There aren't any other options." Not the glowing endorsement for Lavazza's grand mission statement.

I wanted to give the other brands a fair shot, so I asked again. *"What about Amazon and The Pink Stuff?"*

"Amazon is convenient," Maria replied. *"Your Mum recommended the Pink Stuff, and it's cheap."*

"Got it," I said. I saw a pattern emerging. *"What about the mascara and honey?"*

"The mascara doesn't leave black under your eyes. And the honey reminds me of when I lived in the South of France."

"One final question, Maria. Do you know what any of these brands believe or why they do what they do?"

"No idea."

Case closed.

But don't abandon these concepts altogether despite my obvious dislike for the 'Why' cult. Thinking about your values and having a clear mission is essential. When you have clear goals centred on making a positive difference, you develop products people love. But this isn't the same as *"People don't buy what you do. They buy why you do it."* A more accurate sentence is, *"People buy what you do because you think about why you do it."* Granted, it messes up Sinek's Golden Circle, and it won't catch on any time soon. But it's true. When you have an overall focus and direction for your business, you create the right products for the right customers. With that said, let's begin by defining Your World.

Your World comprises the Five V's: Vision, Values, Voice, Visuals, and Vend. I'll admit, 'Vend' is an odd word to use. I would have used 'Products,' but 'Products' doesn't start with a 'v'. And the Four V's and One P isn't memorable. Besides, 'Vend' means "to sell", so it fits—give me a break. Forced acronyms aside, here's a brief definition of each V.

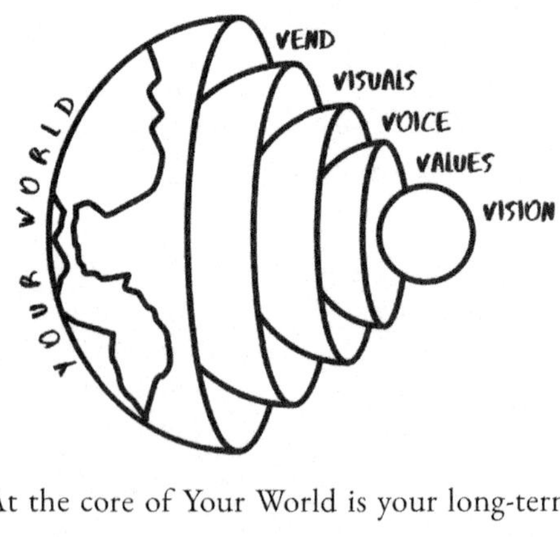

Vision. At the core of Your World is your long-term goal—your mission. Knowing what business you're trying to create for you and your customers makes decision-making more straightforward.

Values. How do you want customers to perceive you and your brand? Communicating your values attracts people who share the same ethos.

If you intend to grow a team around you, they will need to know, understand, and share the company's values.

Voice. Branding runs deeper than logos, colours, and fonts. It extends to your words and the way you communicate. Defining and developing your brand voice is crucial.

Visuals. As you reach the surface of Your World, you must think about customer perceptions. Content that looks like you used '90s Clip Art will turn prospects off. You must create the right visual impression to stand out online. But don't overthink visual branding. You'll discover my 3, 2, 1 method to keep visual branding simple. Even if you don't have an ounce of creativity, you can still create professional content.

Vend. The surface of Your World is where you showcase your products and services. What you're selling should embody your vision, values, voice, and visuals. I'll guide you through developing products your audience can't live without and offers that have them queuing to work with you.

Chapter 5

VISION

The Gravity Method: Your World

"Vision without action is a daydream. Action without vision is a nightmare."

Japanese Proverb

Developing the Gravity Method hasn't been straightforward. I've tested many ideas that turned out to be lousy. I've disappeared down rabbit holes filled with marketing bullshit. I've read book after book on the marketing tactics of Starbucks, Amazon, and Nike. I've turned these strategies into marketing lessons for myself and other coaches. But the concepts never worked. The theory was sound but didn't deliver tangible results in the real world. At least not for the coaches with whom I worked. I'm sure massive corporations need extensive mission-defining exercises. But a company of one? An entrepreneur who employs a Virtual Assistant and, on occasion, hires an agency? It's valuable time that could be better spent elsewhere.

My epiphany came while chatting with my buddy, Austin Current. Austin's a smart guy who gives me the brutal truth in his soft, gentle way. One Tuesday afternoon, we discussed his BHAG (Big Hairy

Audacious Goal). The BHAG is a concept coined by Jim Collins in his book, *Built to Last,*[1] published in 1994. It's the first task my clients *used* to complete before developing a strategy. The premise is simple. Set an ambitious goal with a high probability of failure. In doing so, you'll stretch your limits and reach further than you thought possible. Here are two examples from companies you know and love (or hate).

Starbucks: *"Become the most recognised and respected consumer brand in the world."*

Meta: *"To connect the world."*

Do you get a sense of their ambitious goals from their daily actions? I'll leave you to decide. In the meantime, back to my chat with Austin.

"I dunno, man," Austin said in a cautious tone. I could almost see the cogs whirring in his head as he tried to think of the right words to let me down gently. *"It's just not working for me."*

My translation... *"This is a terrible idea that has no practical value."* Point taken, Austin. I'll have a rethink.

At face value, defining your BHAG sounds great. It's a logical step to create the foundations of a scalable business. To paraphrase Collins, the BHAG stops you thinking too small. A great BHAG creates a sense of urgency. In short, think big. Plan for the long term. Execute with consistency. No problem, Jim. I'm on board. Within days of finishing the book, I had written my BHAG.

---

1. Collins, Jim. (2005). Built To Last: Successful Habits of Visionary Companies

"To connect the world's businesses with their ideal customers."

Pithy. Clear. I liked it. But there was a problem. Fast forward several years, and I've given my lofty goal no thought. I've developed courses, coaching services, and products that have helped hundreds of coaches. My business earned over $100k in the first six months and over $400k in the first two years. But the BHAG I spent so long contemplating had no effect on those outcomes—not one iota. The reality is that your perspective on business and life will change. When faced with a blank balance sheet, it's easy to get carried away with the possibilities ahead. But once you get started, you'll realise it's damn hard work to grow an online business. A more reserved goal could bring you more happiness. My point is that the BHAG teaches you to value more, more, more. But more isn't always better, especially in business. To paraphrase The Notorious B.I.G., more money leads to more problems.

Some marketers will tell you I'm wrong. They'll claim Collins is the G.O.A.T of understanding why and how great companies grow. Are the salivating fanboys right? Sure. It makes sense for bigger organisations. But that's not you or me, so I'll give you three reasons to avoid defining a BHAG.

One. Often, entrepreneurs start their ventures with no marketing skills and no audience. Most don't have a defined product or service that delivers repeatable results. Setting a goal to change the world in the next 25 years borders delusion. Prove your concept and make some initial sales before you get carried away.

Two. Do you need to change the world? The chances of you or I creating a company with hundreds of employees are tiny. Heck. I don't even want that type of business. Give me a company that generates £500k profit over a multimillion-pound stress-inducing beast. You don't need to revolutionise your industry to be successful. Rubbing shoulders with Bezos and Musk while sipping Mai Tais on Waikiki Beach is not your goal. Innovate, yes. Disrupt? Go for it. But don't bank on your little venture transmuting into a global superpower.

Three. Defining your BHAG isn't as straightforward as you might hope. Unless you've got a crystal clear vision from the outset, it takes a lot of thinking time. Even then, there's no guarantee you'll dream up anything meaningful or inspiring. You could spend days—weeks—setting a 25-year goal that you'll abandon six months from now.

And, if you want a fourth reason, here's the coup de grâce: self-doubt. Most entrepreneurs struggle with it. Many never overcome it. In the early days of business, you'll wonder if you're cut out for the job. You'll doubt whether you have the skills to deliver an outstanding service or create a product worth buying. You'll hate the content you create, the emails you send, and the websites you build. As for the sky-high expectations of your BHAG, mental anguish will raze them to the ground in no time.

The alternative is far simpler. It involves setting two distinct goals. One for you. The other for the people whom you want to help.

To help you define success, first, I need to take you back to 2018. I attended a five-day business mastermind with four other coaches. According to the hosts, we would map the path to *"six figures in six months."* (Yes, I was a sucker for lousy marketing back then). Every morning, the event began by holding hands in a circle, chanting affirmations. It was like a low-budget Tony Robbins cult, which I had no desire to join. Of course, the hosts also treated us to various 'expert' speakers across the week. None of whom were experts in anything, as far as I could tell. But this wasn't the most horrific part of the event.

On day one, we had to visualise our perfect day. Like obedient minions, we shut our eyes and listened to the words of our 'expert' teacher. He said this exercise would clarify the actions needed to achieve our dreams. All bets were off. No limitations. *"Let your mind wander"* was the directive. Okay, Mr. Manifestation Guru, hold my imaginary beer.

My day starts in the bedroom of my $4 million beachfront mansion. I'm a stickler for a morning routine, and my perfect day is no different. I wake at 6 a.m. sharp next to a quartet of supermodels: two to the left and two to the right. After obligatory morning coitus, I snort four lines of coke off their inner thighs.

Sniff.

Sniiiff.

Roll over to the right.

Sniiiiiiff.

Sniiiiiiiiiff.

Ahhhh. Then, I throw on my Versace dressing gown and saunter downstairs. I go to the kitchen and catch a whiff of freshly ground Arabica coffee beans. I hear sizzling bacon that's approaching the perfect level of crispness. While sipping espresso and tucking into a bacon sandwich, I check on my businesses, all 40 of them. All is going well. I'm making multibillion-dollar profits, all before 10 am. Life. Is. Grand.

Okay. This isn't my ideal day. It's not even close. But I want to show the ludicrousness of this woo-woo business bullshit. How would any of this help me start an online coaching business? Answer. It won't. But it's the sort of nonsense business gurus tell you is essential if you want success. Trust me. You're wasting your time.

I'm all for ambition and chasing lofty goals. Heck. It's how I ditched a dull corporate job and started my own business. But picturing your perfect day and dusting a vision board in glitter? I'm not buying it. No matter how often you read The Secret, you can't manifest your dreams into existence. It's nonsense. Life is not Field Of Dreams, and you are not Kevin Costner. If you build it, they probably won't come... unless you ditch the woo-woo crap and focus on solid marketing principles.

With defining a BHAG and imagining your perfect day crossed off the list, what should you do? Well, there are two things to consider. What business do you want to create? And what impact do you want to have on your target audience? Let's start with the former.

Are you an introvert who wants to sell online courses and digital products? Do you feed off the energy of others and need in-person interaction? Or, are you an innovator who wants to create an app that revolutionises your industry? The options are endless. But there will be an ideal business for you. Don't let the hustlers sway you. The worst thing you can do is build a business you'll hate in five years.

You might not be able to realise your idyllic vision from day one, but you can evolve towards it. Take my business, Maverick Goose, for example. Despite what you see on social media, I'm an introvert. Too much direct interaction with others is draining. So, my main income streams are online courses and a monthly print newsletter. My 1:1 mentorship is an exclusive club, and I'm strict about how many people I work with and who gets through the door. I know what I enjoy, and I know what leads to burnout. But it wasn't always this way. In the beginning, I concentrated on done-for-you services: content creation and strategy development. I needed to gain experience, understand my market, and make a name for myself. After all, selling online courses without credibility is a tough game. Set your vision, but treat it as the destination, not the starting point.

The second part of your vision is how you will impact your niche. Do you want to rid the world of fad diets? Are you on a mission to make pro-level copy accessible to cash-strapped entrepreneurs? Perhaps you want to create an army of knowledgeable coaches who can impact the world. Heck! Are you the person to bring peace to humanity? Whatever your niche, whatever your goal, having direction is essential. Combine this direction with the type of business you wish to create, and you'll have your vision. Use this "North Star" to influence every decision, action, post, email, sales page, and offer. Ensure everything you do propels your business in this direction. If an idea pops into your head, sense-check it with your vision. And if it doesn't align, ignore it.

I've been around long enough to know that two questions follow when a task requires thinking. *"Have you got a template?"* and *"Can you show me some examples?"* In Part Three, I'll share examples, templates, and frameworks to help develop your marketing strategy, but for this, you're on your own. If it hurts to think. Well, Good! I'm not asking you to share your vision with anyone. You're not going to paint your vision across the walls of the town hall in ten-foot letters. This exercise is for your benefit, no one else's. Giving you templates and examples constrains your thinking. You'll create a cookie-cutter vision that won't mean anything to you. Sure, you'll be happy to tick a box and move on to the next task, but it will be for nothing. So, here's my challenge to you. Spend thirty minutes thinking about the business that would give you passion and drive. Then, think about what impact you want that business to have on the world. Easy.

If you can't do that without a template, close this book and move on with your life. You're going to find the real work of building your business impossible.

Chapter 6

VALUES

The Gravity Method: Your World

"Your brand is what people say about you when you're not in the room."

Jeff Bezos

Starting a section on values with a quote from Amazon founder, Jeff Bezos, might seem strange. (Judging by mainstream media, the whispers in the room aren't favourable, Jeff). But whether you love or loathe Jeff Bezos, the quote is valid.

Before social media and the internet, business owners dictated brand perception. Television, print, and radio advertising were the juggernauts that ruled the marketing world. Through these channels, brands had almost total control over perception. Word of mouth had an effect locally, but not to the extent it does today. The advent of social media, and its 4.4 billion users (and counting), has shifted our buying decisions. People are savvier, more informed, and can easily share their thoughts on a global scale. It's now the public that bestows meaning and status on brands.

Branding is meaning-making—giving your brand purpose. But this meaning is neither owned nor created by you, the business owner; it's signalled. You can scream from the rooftops that you're the best, but you don't decide. It's your audience who decides. All you can do is communicate the right message.

You can't dictate what people should think about your business or anything you sell. It's scary. The only influence you have is through your marketing channels. But even then, this influence is weak. Once you start selling products and posting content, control shifts to your audience. Friends, family, and trusted influencers wield the most power. For example, if a friend tells you a product is lame, would you ignore them and trust the marketing instead? Doubtful.

Branding is a complex beast. Wrapping your head around branding's intricacies can feel like trying to suplex a blue whale.

I'm giving branding a bad wrap, which might lead you to think that branding is worthless. After all, you're not building the next Amazon or Nike. You're an online entrepreneur. You want to sell enough products to live a comfortable life and enjoy the wild ride to the grave. Good news! You don't need an army of branding experts or spend weeks developing a brand strategy. There is a simpler way—a way to BOSS your branding.

- Brand Adjectives and Values
- Own a Word
- Social Media
- Service Delivery

Brand Adjectives and Values

Your goal is to influence brand perception as much as possible. But, to communicate the right message, you must define your values. The most straightforward way to do this is by choosing three brand adjectives. Here are three examples:

- Honest. Fun. Trustworthy.
- Bold. Brash. Stylish.
- Scientific. Dependable. Knowledgeable.

Pick any three adjectives that you want your audience to associate with your business.

The Unique Value System

You may have come across the term Unique Value Proposition (UVP). A UVP is a short statement communicating why people should buy. The Unique Value System (UVS) is different. ***A Unique Value System is a set of values that define a unique approach to solving the problems of a specific niche.***

The Intuitive Eating[1] concept is an example of a UVS. Intuitive Eating comprises ten core principles:

1. Reject the Diet Mentality

---

1. Tribile, Evelyn. (1995). Intuitive Eating: A Revolutionary Anti-Diet Approach

2. Honour Your Hunger
3. Make Peace with Food
4. Challenge the Food Police
5. Discover the Satisfaction Factor
6. Feel Your Fullness
7. Cope with Your Emotions with Kindness
8. Respect Your Body
9. Movement—Feel the Difference
10. Honour Your Health—Gentle Nutrition

Whether you agree with the principles is not the point. The point is how a clear UVS gives its customers an ethos to which they can attach themselves. It creates a tribal mentality. But, a word of warning.

By creating a UVS, you're *not* creating one source of the truth. You are creating one source of the process. Your brand is not a cult, and your aim isn't to brainwash your audience and force them to drink the Kool-Aid. There will always be different ways to reach a goal. Claiming you have all the secrets and that the rest of the world is wrong is hyperbolic. Make legitimate claims. Social media is already a cesspool. So, solve problems. Don't post propaganda.

Start by developing up to seven values that define what you believe and your process. Why seven? Well, George A. Miller, a Harvard Cognitive Psychologist, is an expert on short-term memory. Miller's research concluded that the sweet spot for memory recall was seven (plus or minus two).[2] You see the rule in everyday life without realising. Take your mobile phone number, for example. Imagine your phone number is 1-5726142895. You wouldn't remember this nor tell it to others as one long number.

"What's your phone number? I'd love to go on a second date."

"Sure. it's fifteen billion, seven hundred and twenty-six million, one hundred and forty-two thousand, eight hundred and ninety-five."

"Huh?" Before you have time to think, the door slams in your face, and you're back on the dating apps before sundown.

Most sane people chunk phone numbers into two-to-five-digit sections.

"15726..."

"Uh-huh."

"142...

"Mmmm. Hmmm."

"895..."

Now, you'll be sexting within the hour. All thanks to Miller's Law. And you can apply it to your UVS.

---

2. Miller, G. (1956). The magical number seven, plus or minus two: Some limits on our capacity for processing information. The psychological review, 63, 81-97.

Make your UVS memorable. Don't dream up 25 values. People will zone out and forget your values (and you) exist. The application of Miller's research to these marketing principles isn't tested. It's not science, so I could be wrong. But, the principle of keeping concepts short and memorable is never a bad idea.

Once you define your UVS, post it in a prominent place on social media and weave it into sales pages. The majority of your posts (if not all, in some cases) should relate to these principles. Your audience needs repeated exposure to know they exist.

In Part Three, I'll introduce you to the Unique Mechanism (UM). To avoid confusion, I'll tell you now that the UM and UVS are two different concepts. Think of the Unique Mechanism as the method to help people implement your UVS and initiate positive change.

Own a Word

Consumers often associate Volvo with safety. People choose the boxy Swedes if protecting themselves and their passengers is a priority. But if you value reliability, Lexus might be your first choice. The Japanese manufacturer is at the top of the reliability charts year after year. Brands use these word associations to drive specific marketing messages. Through this process, the car makers carve out a sub-niche they can dominate.

Think about a word you can own in your niche. Are you known for making complex topics simple? If so, you could aim to own 'simplicity.' If you deliver a high-end service, 'Premium' could be an option. The trick is finding a word with little or no competition. Granted, it'll take guesswork. But if you know your niche, making assumptions is fine at this stage.

Social Media

Social Media is the mechanism through which you communicate your message. Every post should embody your brand values. If it doesn't, it's "off-brand" and needs a rethink. Don't lip-sync and copy viral dance routines if you want followers to think you're anything but a clown.

When every video, image, and caption has your values at its core, you send the right signals to your audience. And you edge closer to owning your chosen word with every post.

Service Delivery

Word-of-mouth often starts with the people who buy what you're selling. Give people a fantastic service, and they'll sing your praises and reward you with loyalty. But give them a lousy experience, and their fury and vitriol spread ten times faster. Don't focus on marketing and ignore delivering on your promises. After all... *"Nothing will make a bad product fail faster than good advertising."* - William Berbach.

An ideal way to ensure you deliver a stellar service is threefold.

1. Be good at what you do.

Whether you're helping people lose weight, or giving marketing advice, deliver consistent results. Invest in your knowledge, skills, systems, and processes. Don't sell customers a dream, then give them nightmares once they've paid.

2. Think of customers first.

Every decision should have your audience at heart. Free content, paid products, and new services should always benefit your ideal customers. If they don't, your actions aren't suitable for your brand.

3. Don't just deliver quick wins; get them to the transformation.

Speed of change is critical to longevity. The faster you deliver results, the more money people spend, and the quicker they refer you to others. Start by focusing on what happens after the sale. How can you create a smooth onboarding experience to increase consumption and buy-in?

I've invested in courses and membership sites, only to take a cursory glance at the content. After a few months, I've forgotten they exist and chalk it up to another moment of buying madness. But, with an effective onboarding process, you can avoid this scenario.

Businesses often think that giving more, more, more is the answer. But more leads to overwhelm. Your customer is already up to their eyeballs in information. They came to you because they didn't know what to do, and everything felt too much. They want you to simplify the process. They want you to guide them. Much like Luke Skywalker needed Obi-Wan and Yoda, your customers need a guide. You are not the hero of your customer's story. You are not swooping in to save the day, rescue them from failure, and leave with all the glory and riches.

No, no, no. You are the guide, showing them the way and helping them avoid the pitfalls and defeat their enemies. Your customer is always the hero.

Any hoot, I digress. My point is that simplification is valuable. Complexity is off-putting. When designing your onboarding process, make it as effortless as possible.

Follow the BOSS process, and you'll start to build a tribe of loyal followers. These superfans love every post and buy every product. Not even the biggest advertising budgets in the world can buy this degree of brand loyalty.

Chapter 7

VOICE

The Gravity Method: Your World

"The urge, starting out, is to copy. And that's not a bad thing. Most of us only find our own voices after we've sounded like a lot of other people. But the one thing that you have that nobody else has is you. Your voice, your mind, your story, your vision. The moment you feel that, just possibly, you're walking down the street naked, exposing too much of your heart and your mind and what exists on the inside, showing too much of yourself. That's the moment you may be starting to get it right."[1]

Neil Gaiman

Trying to attract new clients based on your ability to pump out facts is a bold strategy—a *bad*, bold strategy. Creating a stand-out brand takes more than regurgitating the Encyclopedia Britannica. And you'll need a little more charisma than a clump of pocket fluff. Inject your brand with personality and what the French call a certain... I don't

1. Gaiman, Neil. (2012). University of the Arts Keynote Address

know what. Then, your brand takes on a unique character and cuts through social media's white noise.

There are three elements to finding your brand voice. More on those in a second. First, I'll say one thing. Gaiman's words that opened this chapter say everything. Be yourself, but louder. It makes me think of a conversation with my Dad when I was sixteen and applying for my first part-time job.

I was a massive fan of WWE (Professional Wrestling if you don't understand the acronym). It was the 90s, and Stone Cold Steve Austin was one of the WWE's biggest stars. His entrance was iconic. You knew it was go time when you heard the sound of glass breaking. The staccato guitar riff, reminiscent of Rage Against The Machine, sent the crowd wild. Duh-da, Duh-Da, Duh-Da. Then, Stone Cold emerges from behind the curtain, dressed in black. Black boots, black trucks, and a black leather waistcoat emblazoned with skulls. Stone Cold approached the ring with the confident swagger of a man who feared no one. My Dad told me this was the energy I needed to bring to my job interviews. I won't lie. I was dubious.

"Are you saying I should wear biker gear and underwear for an interview at Tesco's?"

"No, son. Don't be stupid." He said in his firm, fatherly tone. *"Bring the confidence. Find that part of your personality and crank it up."*

"Got it, Dad. Thanks for the advice."

My father's advice didn't get me the job, to my utter dismay. Swaggering into the room and nailing the interviewer with a Stone Cold

Stunner is a lousy strategy. Who knew? My Dad's advice is better suited to social media marketing than job interviews. I'll explain.

You wouldn't think it to look at my content, but I'm an introvert. I'm the guy who hates social gatherings. I avoid them at all costs. But, if I'm at a social event, you'll find me at the back of the room, nursing the same drink in silence. And I'll only speak to the people who decide to take pity on me. I'm not being rude. It's more that it takes a lot of emotional energy to mingle and chit-chat. And most of the time, my social batteries run low.

Getting in front of the camera to make content was a mammoth event. I hated it. Every time I watched the videos back, they were devoid of personality. It wasn't me delivering the tips and insights. It was an imposter—a Simon clone sent to send my audience to sleep. These days, I recall the conversation with my Dad before creating content. I tap into the confident extrovert buried deep inside and crank it up to eleven. *"Oi! You! Give me my leather waistcoat and hit the music. I've got content to make."*

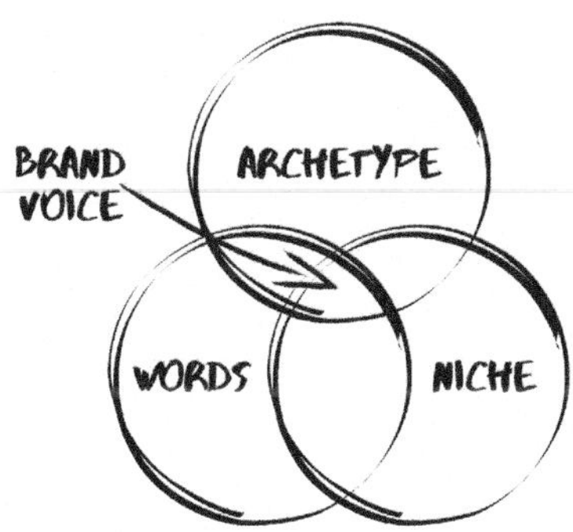

The point is you can create a brand identity by being yourself. I'll describe brand archetypes, niche-voicing, words, and references. But, to be honest. If you can be yourself but one louder, you'll be fine.

Brand archetypes

Prospects want to know what you believe and what you stand for. They want to see congruence between those values and the messages you communicate. Customers want to know if your brand is a tribe they can trust.

Well-known companies infuse trust and consistency into their brands using archetypes (allegedly). And through subtle actions, brands create a tribe of like-minded, die-hard customers.

"Archetypes help us to understand the intrinsic meaning of product categories and consequently help marketers create enduring brand identity that can establish market dominance, evoke and deliver meaning to customers, and inspire customer loyalty." – Carol Pearson & Margaret Mark, The Hero and the Outlaw.[2]

There are twelve brand archetypes, which are as follows:

1. The Innocent – Example: Dove.

Desires to provide happiness and do the right thing.

2. The Sage – Example: BBC.

---

2. Pearson, Carol and Mark, Margaret (2001). The Hero and the Outlaw: Building Extraordinary Brands Through The Power of Archetypes.

Seeks knowledge, wisdom, and truth.

3. The Explorer – Example: Land Rover.

Yearns for freedom and adventure.

4. The Outlaw – Example: Harley Davidson.

The rebel. The rule breaker.

5. The Magician – Example: Disney.

A strong belief in making dreams come true. Example: Disney.

6. The Hero – Example: Nike.

There to motivate, inspire, and encourage.

7. The Lover – Example: Chanel.

Sensual. Focused on emotional and physical appeal.

8. The Jester – Example: Dollar Shave Club.

Brings fun and playfulness to all situations.

9. The Citizen – Example: Ford.

Relatable and down to earth. For regular people.

10. The Ruler – Example: Rolex.

Excudes power, craves control and exclusivity.

11. The Caregiver – Example: NHS.

A genuine passion for helping and caring for others.

12. The Creator – Example: Apple

Innovators and creative problem solvers.

But brand archetypes are not without their critics. Marketing Professor Mark Ritson once gave the concept a scathing critique.

"Total bollocks but incredibly prevalent... I've met scores of companies who have asked me to explain what they are meant to do with this stuff, and I've always given the same advice. Bin it."[3]

Who's right, and who's wrong? I'm no marketing professor, but I side with Ritson... almost. Trying to pigeonhole your brand into a strict framework seems banal. After all, you're trying to stand out, so why force yourself to become tethered to a set of rules that don't quite fit?

Apple is often considered The Creator. Apple leads the charge with innovation and telling the world to *"think different."* But you could make a strong case that Apple also fits The Outlaw archetype. The Outlaw is a rebel, a rogue on a mission to shake things up and get people to... errr... *"think different."* You could also say Apple is The Explorer. Explorer Brands want freedom and aren't restricted by typical boundaries. They... errr... *"think different."*

There's a pattern emerging.

It's problematic to assign your brand an archetype if doing so constrains your thinking. You're in danger of limiting possibilities and

---

3. Ritson, Mark. (2020). 'Humaning' and the greatest marketing bullshit of all time. marketingweek.com

second-guessing all you do. But I'm not ready to throw the idea away altogether.

You can use brand archetypes to establish your brand's primary ethos. It's not fixed and never set in stone. It's a general direction to which you gravitate. Mix the components of your chosen archetype with your personality and brand. It will mean your brand won't fit into a pre-defined category, but that's not such a bad thing.

Maverick Goose is The Outlaw. A Maverick flies in the face of the norm and goes their own way. But Maverick Goose is also The Creator, The Jester, The Innocent, and a little of every archetype. But The Outlaw is my "North Star." I ensure I'm bringing new ideas to social media marketing where existing ones are weak and outdated. Then, I allow other aspects of my personality to emerge—unrestricted. It's this blend that gives my brand both purpose and personality.

Use brand archetypes if they resonate with you. Think about the specific signals you want to send to your ideal customers. Do you want to be the techie geek into scientific detail? Or are you the down-to-earth educator, simplifying concepts when others choose to complicate? But if archetypes make no difference to your brand and marketing, don't waste your time. As Ritson says, *"Bin it."*

Niche and Words

As you produce more content, your audience develops expectations. Bring consistency to your tone and style to deliver a congruent marketing message. Ensure your words, phrases, and references match your desired brand perception. Your aim is to make your avatar feel like you made every post for them and only them.

Your words must also match your ethos. If I used timid, play-it-safe language, it wouldn't suit the rebellious direction of the brand. Look at successful personal brands, and you'll see the same congruence.

Gary Vaynerchuk, Mark Manson, and James Smith are bold, brash, and direct. It's an attitude prevalent throughout their words, videos, and content. In contrast, Dr Julie Smith and Alex Hormozi have a sympathetic, educative style.

But don't overcomplicate finding your voice. The examples I've used are all people who are being themselves online. So, the quicker you unleash your personality, the quicker you find your brand voice.

Chapter 8

VISUALS

The Gravity Method: Your World

"Design is the servant of the written word."

William Zissner

It was a bright, sweltering day in August, and I was scribbling like a madman on the whiteboard. I felt like I'd cracked the content code. My frantic scrawl revealed my entire content strategy with each pen stroke. This was the whole process. Everything from ideation to creation. I delved into the sneaky efficiency tricks that kept me omnipresent across several platforms. This was the first time I'd explained the entire process to anyone. My friends Ross and Mal recorded every word I said.

It all started with "Hero Content." Hero Content was the primary content from which I extracted all my social media posts. Content creation started with a long-form article. I would publish the article on my website and several online platforms. Then, I would read the article aloud, recording the audio and visuals for YouTube and my podcast. I'd create a summary of the article for a carousel-style Instagram post. I converted each article section into a post and highlighted quotes to repost as tweets. One article provided content for almost all the prominent platforms. After speaking for over an hour, I turned around to see what Mal and Ross thought. Their expressions were a mix of amazement and confusion.

"Does it make sense?" I asked, trying to gauge whether I'd put them off content creation for life. *"Have you got any questions?"*

The response to this question lives on as a standing joke between the three of us. And there's no better way to show you the twisted logic of most online business owners.

"What about the colours?" Mal replied.

"The colours? The colours?" Mal, I love you, but come on. You could've focused on any aspect of the process, and you chose colours!

Mal is my best friend, so she won't mind me telling you she is obsessed with colours. Several times since *"Colourgate"*, we've discussed content strategy, sales funnels, and email marketing. I've told her, in detail, about crafting hooks and how to write a compelling call-to-action. But I guarantee her first response will always be, *"...but what about the colours?"* It's as if the way to unlock more leads and growth is a new shade of mauve. But Mal isn't the only one. Hundreds of online entrepreneurs have taken my Social Launch course. How many people fuss over colour choices and font pairings still amazes me. Of course, it matters, but make no mistake, the message is more important than the mechanism. What you say is more important than how you say it. A turd boxed and wrapped in gorgeous decorative paper is still a turd. Whereas people will fight to unearth a 5-carat diamond embedded in poop. This doesn't mean design is unimportant. Good luck getting leads if your content resembles a five-year-old's finger painting.

I could spend the next 2,000 words teaching you colour theory (I won't). I considered guiding you through analogous, monochromatic, and complementary colours. But I can't imagine you'd ever use the information. I even thought about giving you a brief history of colours and their ideal use. I mean, who doesn't want to learn the history of magenta? Or that amber has associations with energy? These insights are invaluable for your marketing decisions, right? Well, no. Instead of useless theory, I'll guide you through my simple "3, 2, 1 Method." It's much more your speed.

The 3, 2, 1 Method

The 3, 2, 1 Method is simple:

- Three Colours
- Two Fonts
- One Logo

Colours:

For reasons I don't recall, I wanted my company name to include an animal. This kickstarted a bizarre train of thought. Blue Donkey, Blue Mule, and Crazy Cow were all names I considered. Proof that even the best of us start with lousy ideas. Nothing clicked until one day, I decided to rewatch the movie Top Gun. For the uninitiated, Maverick was the call sign of Tom Cruise's character in the film. Goose was his best friend and co-pilot. Goose ticked the box of my desire to have an animal in the brand name. Maverick means 'unorthodox', 'rebellious', and independent thinker. I felt like a Maverick thinker, going against the grain of modern social media marketing. It was perfect.

With the name locked in, the creative cogs started turning. I took a screenshot of Maverick's red, white, and blue helmet and uploaded it to my design software. I chose the exact colour tones of the helmet for my visual branding. From there, I decided to lean into the aviation theme even more. I started calling my followers Social Mavericks and used the same name for my community. Presentations looked like mission briefings. And my print newsletter looked like a top-secret dossier. One simple idea sparked an entire brand. But the idea didn't come from a brainstorm. It didn't spring to mind by locking myself in a darkened room, praying for something usable. My brand originated from taking a break and allowing myself to absorb inspiration. Sometimes, you need to mix the 3-2-1 framework with organic ideas for which you can't legislate. As the great movie director Orson Welles said of the creative process, "*...we go fishing for accidents.*"[1] The point is, if inspiration doesn't hit you like a bolt of lightning after reading the following paragraphs, don't panic. Take a step back and allow yourself space for the ideas to come to you as if it was one of Welles's "divine accidents."

The simple approach is to pick three colours: dark, light, and accent. That's it. And if you want to keep it even more basic, choose black, white, and your favourite accent colour. Don't make it any more complicated. When your business is making millions, hire a top marketing agency to choose the right shade of grey. They'll even tell you what

---

1. Welles, Orson. (2018). They'll love me when I'm dead. Dir. Morgan Neville.

shade evokes the right emotions in consumers. (At least that's what they'll say to you to justify the eye-watering invoice). Until then, don't worry about it. You'll get leads and make sales as long as your colour palette isn't visual cyanide. Pick three colours and stick to them.

As the old adage goes, "Less is more." Amateur designs are easy to spot because the creator didn't know when to stop. Constraining yourself to three colours keeps your designs consistent and reduces thinking time. Choosing a new set of colours for every post is both needless and stupid. After all, consistent visual branding creates familiarity with your audience. When your content appears in their feed, simple visual cues like colours and fonts help them identify your content within the mass of posts crammed into their feed. This means your audience is much more likely to pay attention to your message. But when your posts look random, you don't create these associations and miss vital opportunities to nurture your followers toward a sale.

Fonts:

There are three simple rules for selecting your two fonts.

1. The headline font must be versatile and readable.

2. The body font must be easily read in various sizes.

3. The fonts must suit the brand.

Attention is the true currency of social media. When you grab (and hold) attention, you increase the likelihood of leads and sales. Font choice plays a small but crucial part in the process. Your headline font must be readable. This isn't the place for decorative, handwritten fonts. You won't grab attention if no one can read the headline. The

"Father of Advertising," David Ogilvy, reiterated this point when he said,

"On average, five times as many people read the headlines as read the body copy. It follows that unless your headline sells your product, you have wasted 90% of your money."[2]

His quote refers to what the headline says rather than the font choice, but the point still applies. If the headline doesn't grab attention, everything else you wrote or said was a waste of time. So, don't sacrifice your chances of success by choosing an unreadable headline font.

The body font is easier to choose. Pick anything. I'm serious. If you can read it in all font sizes and it suits your brand, go for it. This approach might seem too simplistic. If typography was this simple, why are there rows of books on the topic in every bookshop? Those authors who write 250+ pages on the correct use of serif fonts and font pairings must know something I don't. Well, I'm sure they have valid points. But the book you're reading is for non-designers. It's for people who want leads and sales from social media. It's not for those who like to pontificate about majuscules, ascenders, the axis, and the swash. The only thing you should care about at this stage is readability.

There are two main font styles from which to choose. The first is a "serif" typeface. Serif fonts include small lines or strokes attached to the ends of larger strokes. For example, if you're reading the print version of this book, you'll be reading a serif typeface. This is because the general consensus is serif fonts are easier to read in print. The second option is a "sans serif" typeface. These fonts don't have small

---

2. Ogilvy, David. (1985). Ogilvy On Advertising.

lines attached to individual letters. Hence, they are without (sans) the serif. Sans Serif typefaces are often considered easier to read on digital platforms. The difference is minor but worth considering.

The last rule of font choice is suitability. Your fonts must suit your brand. Remember the section on brand values? You didn't skip it, did you? Suppose your three brand adjectives were stylish, elegant, and sophisticated. In this case, don't choose a font that would look at home on the cover of a Marvel comic. It doesn't fit. Likewise, if you want a fun, humorous, and brash brand, don't look to Rolex and Prada for font inspiration. As with most things, a little common sense goes a long way.

Here's a tip if you're struggling to decide on the right font pairing. Do what every self-respecting entrepreneur with better things to do does... Google it. Search for "font pairings"; I guarantee you'll discover countless articles with suggestions. Pick one and move on with your life. We have more important things to cover. Your logo isn't one of those important things, so I'll skim through this topic in two paragraphs.

Logos:

You don't need a logo—at least not in the beginning. It's a needless consideration for most online service businesses until you're more established. No one ever invested in a service business because of the logo. Worry about making money, not whether your logo will look snazzy on a t-shirt. There are obvious exceptions. Logo designers, please send your hate mail to simon@youdontneedalogo.com.

But let's assume you're getting leads, making sales, and want to increase brand awareness. A professional logo will give your brand a unique identity. I'm not a logo designer, so I only have one piece of advice. Use a professional designer. Don't skimp on costs or think about doing it yourself. You'll end up with a logo resembling '90s Clip Art. Your logo is the visual representation of your business, so don't make it a cheap afterthought.

Final thoughts on visual branding:

Branding is not your colour palette or font choice. Yes, it's part of the equation, but it's not your primary focus. Creating a brand that makes money requires all the components of The Gravity Method. For example, beautiful designs count for nothing if you don't understand your niche. The truth is, you don't need beautiful designs to make sales on social media. It helps, sure. Adding great design to a stellar message is always beneficial. But remember, the message is more important than the mechanism.

Chapter 9

VEND

The Gravity Method: Your World

"Money isn't the most important thing in life, but it's reasonably close to oxygen on the 'gotta have it' scale."

Zig Ziglar

In my younger and more naive years, a friend gave me some advice that has been imprinted in my mind ever since. *"The offer is everything."* A clear, simple, well-crafted, unique offer generates sales. A confusing, generic offer is a recipe for lousy returns. But despite heeding these wise words, I've often hit 'The Offer Wall.'

It's July 2021, one month after my most successful product launch to date. Canva Content Mastery 2.0, my design course, exceeded £20k in revenue in the first week of sales. Modest success in comparison to entrepreneurs who rave about their six-and-seven-figure launches. But, for me, this was like hitting a million-dollar jackpot in Vegas. And I wanted more. I started thinking about how to leverage the successful launch. How could I create more products and offers these people would buy? I sent a short survey to customers who had purchased the course. I asked, *"How else can I help solve your most significant chal-*

lenge?" One suggestion (with subtle variations) appeared in dozens of replies.

Customers loved the course. It simplified creating professional-looking content. But it wasn't a complete solution to solving their biggest headache: getting leads. People wanted and needed more. The most common request was to create a community where I could provide ongoing support. So, two months later, in September 2021, I launched the first iteration of Social Mavericks.

Social Mavericks earned £11,993 during the initial launch. Not bad, but it felt like a failure after the high of Canva Content Mastery 2.0. The following six months highlighted the flaws in my offer.

I couldn't fathom why Social Mavericks memberships weren't skyrocketing every month. The group had everything: group coaching calls, online courses, unlimited Q&A, and monthly live training. Plus, it was a bargain at £199 a month. It amazed me that prospects couldn't see the value in Social Mavericks. And it got worse before it got better.

You expect customer churn in a membership community. It goes with the territory. But I wasn't bringing in enough new members to offset those who decided to leave. I knew I had the wrong offer but didn't know what to change. So, I did what I tell all my clients to do, ask. The responses made the problem clear. I was overwhelming people with too much content. Members loved the courses, the training, and the ability to ask questions. The trouble was that they didn't have time to consume everything. So, they felt left behind—overwhelmed. Members who decided to stay pleaded for a simple process to guide them through the content. I needed to tell people where to start, what to make a priority, and provide a blueprint for success. I went back to the drawing board and created the process that spawned this book.

I knew that if people followed the Posts to Profits process, they would get leads and sales from social media. So, I repackaged the Social Mavericks content into a new offer. Out went the monthly membership subscription. In came an eight-week guided course built around the Posts to Profits framework. I called the course Social Launch, and true to its name, sales took off.

Social Launch generated £25,502 in its first launch. More than double the revenue of the community. It left me both thrilled and confused. The content and price (£498 for 8 weeks) were identical. The only difference was the way I packaged the offer. I had taken a sledgehammer to the Offer Wall and crafted an offer people wanted to buy.

I'll be clear. The Offer Wall *isn't* an issue if your content doesn't attract ideal customers. And it's a dot in the distance if you have weak nurture processes. You only hit the Offer Wall when you do almost everything right. You publish content hyper-focused on your niche. You create lead magnets that grow an email list of ideal clients. You write entertaining, compelling emails your subscribers can't wait to open. And you even design a sales page that piques intrigue in your solution. But you're in a frustrating dead spot. Prospects want to buy from you but don't want what you're selling. You're not making an offer that leaves them saying, *"Yes, yes, yes. Take my money now!"* Instead, prospects think, *"Hmmm. I'll think about it."*

Breaking down the Offer Wall is not always straightforward. Many online entrepreneurs resort to desperate tactics and start slashing prices. But a short-term boost in cash flow often comes at the expense of longevity. Good news! There's an alternative way to create compelling offers. You can smash through the Offer Wall with my 5-step stand-out offer wrecking ball.

The 5 Steps For Stand-Out Offers:

- Define the thing.
- Position the thing.
- Name the thing.
- Price the thing.
- Sell the thing.

There are two other elements to a stand-out offer. One of which requires an entire book of its own—Launch the thing. And the other relates to what happens after the sale—Care about the people buying the thing. If there's ever a Posts to Profits: Volume II, I'll cover these in more detail.

Define the thing

The most basic aspect of your compelling offer is deciding what customers get. It sounds simple, but many businesses butcher their offers at the earliest stage. Defining your offer requires more thought than listing its features. Trust me. I've worked in the fitness industry, where every coaching offer is almost identical.

"I offer bespoke training programmes and personalised nutrition," the coach's website reads. *"You'll access your workouts through my easy-to-use app,"* it continues. And as if it wasn't generic enough, here comes the kicker... *"You'll even get weekly check-ins and access to the private online community."* It's the same offer regurgitated thousands of times across social media. Training programmes, calorie counting, and bastardised versions of James Clear's Atomic Habits principles. Predictable. Predictable. Predictable. Don't get me wrong. Fitness coaches are not alone. In almost every online service-based niche, you'll find similar cookie-cutter offers.

Approaching your offer this way seals the fate of your business before you start. You will never win a race to the bottom. There will always be someone with deeper pockets willing to go cheaper to grab market share. You may make a few sales from close friends and several sympathetic followers, but it won't last. Time is ticking. Soon you'll be scrambling for leads and resorting to spammy marketing tactics. And so starts the slow implosion of your online business. Instead of doing what everyone else does, revisit your Problem Path.

The Problem Path defines your prospect's current state and the goal they want to achieve. The problems between these two points are the basis of your content strategy (more on that later). But they serve another crucial purpose. Smart online businesses turn problems into service solutions. I'll use the online fitness coaching example to explain.

Instead of: ***Bespoke Training Programme.***

The offer could be ***The Lean On Your Lunch Break 30-Minute Workout System.***

One sounds dull. The other sounds like a solution to a specific problem—office workers who lack the time to train. I'll give you another example.

One thing online entrepreneurs hate (unless they're copywriters) is writing sales pages. Writing is hard. Writing persuasive, engaging sales copy feels borderline impossible for most people. But, many new businesses can't afford a decent copywriter, so they must learn the hard way. Imagine you've created a course teaching a newbie how to write better sales copy. Your offer could include ***150 video tutorials and over 75 hours of content.***

But that would be a marketing mistake. A detailed, in-depth course sounds impressive until you realise what problem you're solving. In this example, your prospect is already overwhelmed and is screaming for you to simplify copywriting. These people don't want a mammoth course they'll never complete. Imagine if you could rejig your offer to: ***Discover 80% of everything you need to know about sales copy in under an hour.*** It's clear which offer prospects will buy.

The point is simple. Meet the prospect where they are at, and design your offer around solving problems. Don't have a long list of random features that lack cohesion.

The second aspect of your offer you must consider is 'Time to Value.' This is a concept I'll revisit in greater detail in the next section of the book. But I'll cover the basics here because it's relevant to your offer.

People buy things for two primary reasons. First, we have problems preventing us from achieving goals. You might be overweight and desperate for a six-pack. You might have lousy marketing, terrible copy, and struggle to make online sales. Whatever your immediate challenge, you seek solutions. Second, we want solutions that speed up the change process and make that change easier. No one wants to invest in a service that requires massive effort and takes a lifetime to produce results. So, 'Time to Value' is critical. How long will it take your customer to see an impact, and how much effort will it take? The longer the 'Time to Value' and the greater the effort, the less enticing the offer. The copywriting example above highlights this point. Spending 75 hours wading through tutorials is unappealing. But an hour's blast through almost everything you need to know to start making the cash register ring? Well, sign me up now.

Time to Value matters, but never lie to make more sales. Don't tell people they can achieve all their hopes and dreams in two weeks without lifting a finger. Mistruths will kill your business in a heartbeat. Instead, push yourself to create a unique offer that gets customers from A to B faster and easier.

Position the thing

Some entrepreneurs swear blind it's impossible to get leads from social media.

"Instagram only promotes accounts that spend money on ads."

"The platforms gear everything to favour influencers and celebrities."

"I'm shadowbanned."

Excuse my French. I call connerie. Often, those complaining are posting sporadic, irrelevant content. The same people promote lousy offers no one wants to buy. It's no wonder they experience lacklustre results. Random content, terrible offers, and no strategy inspire nothing but apathy. Part of the problem is positioning (or lack of it).

Most entrepreneurs think positioning and niching are one and the same. Listen to any scam business coach, and they'll tell you to scribble an *"I help..."* statement on the back of a napkin. *"It's all you need,"* they say with brash confidence as if you're wasting time trying to be unique. *"Whack that on your social media profile, and you're set."* But you're far from set. This isn't positioning. It's a generic tick-box exercise that does little to benefit your business.

The mistake entrepreneurs make is they position their business, not what they sell. When you're a solopreneur, your audience doesn't care about your company. This doesn't mean they don't care about you or what you're selling, though. Take my business, Maverick Goose Ltd, for example. Most of my customers don't know this is my company's name. Unless they spot it on an invoice or my email address, I never mention it. But I guarantee they know *my* name. My audience follows the personality behind the brand and the solutions I provide. It's the same all over social media. Look at any business with a social media account for their company and one for their founder. Almost always, the founder's personal profile has more engagement and followers. (The exception is when the founder is worth billions and is never on social media). Perfect positioning lets customers understand what you're selling and why it's unique. Most important of all, you give them a reason to care. Position what you sell because that's what your prospects care about most.

It's no surprise that I love an acronym. It helps me (and you) structure concepts into manageable, understandable processes. Positioning is no different. It was an accident, but my acronym spells... Well, you'll see what it spells.

- Competitor Analysis
- Unique Mechanism
- Niche Category
- Turn Features into Focal Points

At least the acronym served its purpose by being unforgettable.

Competitor Analysis

Market research is tedious but essential. Despite what abundance gurus say, you have competition. I don't care if you chant morning affirmations in the mirror. I don't care if you believe that you can manifest success. More so than ever, your prospects have options. And options mean competition. Your service is not the only choice prospects are considering. This realisation shouldn't scare you into a scarcity mentality. It's a wake-up call. You must position your offer to help people understand why it's different. Otherwise, you're blind to reality and on a collision course with the Offer Wall.

Start with an assessment of your competitors. Put yourself in your prospect's shoes. You have a specific problem and a desired goal. Type

"How to [insert problem or goal]..." into Google, Instagram, Facebook, or wherever your prospects spend time online. What options does your search yield? Many niches have solutions spanning everything from online courses to complete done-for-you services. Think about books, in-person consultations, group coaching, and 1:1 mentorships. Whatever your prospect's budget, there's almost always a solution. Your aim is to position your offer in the "Arena of Alternatives." But don't forget your fiercest competitor. The beast every online entrepreneur must slay, regardless of niche. Apathy. Doing nothing is a real option for your prospects. In fact, it's the most common choice. Working towards a goal can involve hard, time-consuming work; it takes effort. Often, the effort is too much, and staying the same is less painful than change. So, people make a willful decision to abandon success.

Make a list of the best alternatives within each type of solution. For example, what's the best book, group coaching programme, and online course? Next, make an unbiased assessment of each option's strengths and weaknesses. It might not be possible to assess every aspect of every offer but do your best. Now, list the features of your service that match or exceed these strengths. Do the same for the elements of your offer that provide a credible fix for the weaknesses.

Scan the entire document and circle the unique features of your service. Identify what you're doing that no one else is doing. This is the foundation of what makes your offer unique. But you need proof. Loose claims about 'great customer service' and 'unrivalled quality' are meaningless. Your opinion of your own strengths is irrelevant without evidence. Why is your service better than the alternative? Prove it, and match these attributes with specific benefits for your customers.

Now for the critical part that most people miss. List the genuine weaknesses of your offer. Trust me, despite what you may think, your service has flaws. My services have flaws, even now. My 1:1 mentorship is expensive. The price is double, sometimes triple, what you might pay someone else. It's ten times more costly than a group coaching programme. I know it, and I own it. I'm also not an expert in sales call techniques. It's why I don't cover it in this book. Being self-aware of limitations allows me to have honest sales conversations. I can say...

> ***"My 1:1 mentorship is expensive, and it's not for everyone. Heck! It's 2X, 3X, and sometimes 10X more than the competition. But I price it this high because I deliver massive returns on that investment. Take Dan, for example..."***

Owning your weaknesses puts you in a position of strength. You soften the blow for your prospects by bringing flaws to the fore. If potential customers go fishing for the "catch" and find it, you lose valuable sales.

Unique Mechanism

Online service-based businesses often stumble headfirst into the *"Rolling Monthly Pitfall."* Recurring revenue eases the pressure of generating new sales every month. But pitching a never-ending monthly subscription with no definitive milestones is a mistake. People want a process to follow. As Donald Miller says in his book,

Building A Storybrand[1] , people want a guide. Luke Skywalker had Yoda, and Frodo had Gandalf. In all great hero stories, the protagonist is the one who faces adversity. The would-be warrior has a mission but lacks the necessary skills and experience. Enter the guide—the saviour sent to light the path to victory over the enemy. The wizened, often weather-beaten master has been there and done it before. The guide knows the road ahead through trials and tribulations—they have a plan. Now, they must show their prodigy the way. You are the Gandalf—the Yoda—of your customer's story. Your prospect is the hero, and your sole job is to guide them to glory. So, you must have a clear, tangible process for success—a unique mechanism.

"But my process is bespoke for every client," is the typical retort I hear. *"Everyone is different."* It's true. Everyone is different. Everyone has unique circumstances, starting points, and challenges. But this doesn't prevent you from creating a marketable process your audience understands. Take the Posts to Profits process, for example.

Posts to Profits works for online service-based businesses across many industries. Some are in the planning and pre-launch phase and don't know where to begin. Others have been in business for years but struggle to grow online revenue. Despite being at opposite ends of the spectrum, Posts to Profits works. The difference is the speed with which a business progresses through the process. A well-established company might have the basics in place. In this instance, I would sense-check everything and move on once I've ticked every box. Conversely, a business in its infancy might have nothing in place.

---

1. Miller, Donald. (2017). Building a Storybrand: Clarify Your Message So Customers Will Listen.

The starting point is the same, but I would spend longer—weeks or months—implementing the basics.

Rewind the clock to my days as an online fitness coach, and you'll see a similar approach. I marketed my body transformation programme using The Lean Life Method. The Lean Life Method was my five-phase unique mechanism.

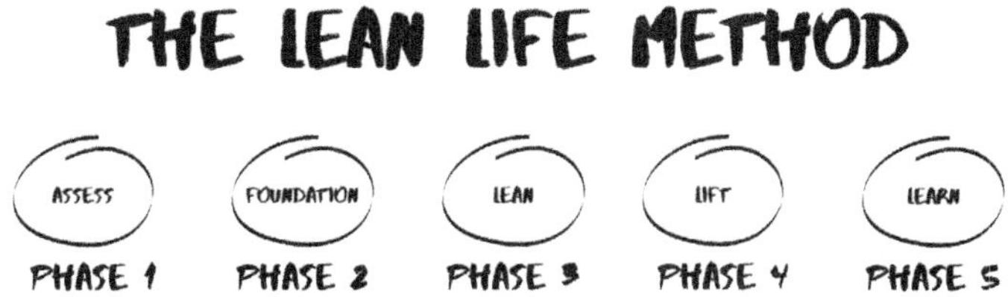

Clients started with an Assessment. This included an onboarding questionnaire, food diary, and form check. The goal was to understand the current situation and identify quick wins. The next phase focused on foundations, as my clients were often new to proper diet and exercise. I combined simple nutrition and habit changes with a basic training programme. Then, with solid foundations, clients moved on to Phases 3-5: Lean, Lift, Learn. 'Lean' was a fancy way of saying 'diet'. 'Lift' was the synonym for building muscle. 'Learn' was the stage where clients learned how to maintain results for life. The beauty of the Lean Life Method was that I could adjust the duration and content within the phases. It kept coaching personalised but within the same broad framework.

Social media leads come far easier when you create a *"secret sauce."* For example, let's assume the Posts to Profits process makes perfect sense to you. You've consumed my social media content and aligned with my approach. You're convinced the step-by-step process is what you need, and you want more. Well, there's only one source of information. Me. Sure, business coaches will try to rip off my process. Heck! By the time you finish reading this book, I expect the salient points to be all over social media. But like a cheap imitation handbag, there's no substitute for the real thing. A unique mechanism gives you leverage within your niche. Do you need a unique mechanism? No. But it removes many of the marketing headaches you're experiencing. Map out your process, name it, depict it, and market it.

Niche Category

We've covered niching to find your ideal client, so I won't revisit old ground. But, there's an added component to niching that applies to your offer. First, aim to position your offer based on the characteristics of loyal customers. What makes your products and services so appealing to these people? Focus on the small percentage who buy without question or hankering for a discount. Think of these customers when creating videos, captions, and sales pages. You'll attract the best buyers more often.

Second, choose your words with care. Prospects create assumptions and associations based on the way you describe your service. If I describe my service as "an online community," people make comparisons. Their subconscious mind anchors their thoughts based on previous knowledge of communities. Price is one example. Online communities often range from between £10 to £99 a month (yes, there are communities priced much higher). If I priced an online community at £997 a month, I risk creating cognitive dissonance. The price doesn't align with expectations, which creates doubt and fear. And you don't need me to tell you that doubt and fear don't sell.

Choosing the proper description for your service also works to your advantage. You can skip explaining every feature because there is a degree of assumption. You can also pit yourself against competitors who lack your offer's unique characteristics.

Third, you must decide where to position your service against the competition. Defining your niche will do the heavy lifting, but it's worth pausing here to reflect. After all, you may want to change tack, having thought about product positioning. There are three niche categories. These options range from broad to narrow.

Head to Head: This is the broadest and toughest niche category. It's where the market leader sits atop their throne. Most online businesses should steer clear of competing at this level. You're up against much larger companies with much larger advertising budgets. You might think you can usurp the leader. But if you refuse to listen to me, listen to the King of Direct Marketing, Dan Kennedy. *"Whoever can spend the most money to acquire a customer wins."*[2]

Big Fish, Small Pond: Most online entrepreneurs end up here. It's logical. Carve out a subsegment of an existing market, stand out, and dominate. Well, this is the logic. It's easier said than done, though. Targeting a sub-niche allows you to become the go-to person for a smaller population. You can target buyers with specific needs that the market leader can't meet with a broad solution.

Create a New Niche: This is the most lucrative and difficult niche category to crack. The idea is to create your own niche and position

---

2. Kennedy, Dan. (2023). At the bottom of every marketing email he sends.

your solution as the only option. Crack the code, and with no competition, sales are a cinch. But it's hard to achieve. Even if you have an innovative offer, selling your solution isn't straightforward. You must prove to customers that a new market category deserves to exist. Not easy.

Whatever niche category you choose, there's one general principle to follow. The broader the niche, the harder it is, and the more it'll cost to stand out. The narrower the niche, the easier it is, and the less it'll cost to stand out. Of course, there are exceptions, but the rule applies to most online businesses. The image below shows this principle for the marketing niche.

One last point. The more authority and notoriety you have within your niche, the broader the niche you can target.

Turn Features Into Focal Points

I have a miniature Dachshund, Randy. He's a dog who lives life on the edge. But when I say he lives life on the edge, I mean on the edge of a nervous breakdown. Everything scares Randy. Dogs, people, cars, buses, bikes, flies, umbrellas, even wind. I've taken him to a doggy therapist to try and ease his anxiety, but nothing works. Unless he's at home in complete silence, he's anxious. You can see his fear come to the fore when a stranger tries to give him a treat. In the beginning, he's curious. Watch close, and you'll see the cogs whirring in his head. He's weighing up the promise of a treat with his anxiety that something terrible might happen. Make a sudden move, and he'll bolt. Allow him to come to you, and he'll swipe the treat and be rolling on his back, pleading for you to rub his belly. This balance of curiosity and anxiety is something we experience during buying decisions. An offer intrigues us, so we lean in, eager to learn more. We love novelty—so the temptation of something new is strong. But our anxiety peaks if the offer is too different. Not wanting to make a wrong decision or worsen our current situation, we often do nothing. Author Oren Klaff says, *"In practice, too much novelty produces avoidance and not the hoped-for attraction effect."*[3]

Klaff also provides the solution. *"The trick is to use a technique called Novelty Chunking,"* he states. *"...make it seem like your deal is different from "normal" in just one key way..."*[4] The point is, make your offer different, but not too different. Then, make the differentiating factor a core focal point of your marketing.

You're almost at the end of the positioning process. All this work. All this background research and analysis comes down to one sentence. And it starts, *"Only I..."*

---

3. Klaff, Oren (2019). Flip The Script: Getting People to Think Your Idea Is Their Idea, pg 99.

4. Klaff, Oren (2019). Flip The Script: Getting People to Think Your Idea Is Their Idea, pg 122.

The "Only I..." statement is a form of a Unique Selling Proposition (USP). It's not an elevator pitch, more an elevator description. The aim is to position your service in people's minds in less than thirty seconds. It also helps you answer the question, "Why buy from you? Here's mine.

Only I have used a decade of marketing experience to create the Posts to Profits Process. It's a unique content marketing system designed for social media. It helps online service-based businesses generate consistent leads and sales.

If you've followed my positioning process, you've created a unique space in the marketplace for your offer. You, dear reader, have positioned your offer like a C.U.N.T.

Name The Thing

"In the positioning era, the single most important marketing decision you can make is what to name the product."[5] So say the great Al Ries and Jack Trout in their classic marketing book, Positioning.

Who am I to argue? The name of your product or service is often the prospect's first interaction with it. If the name is lousy, it'll be the last reaction. A strong product name creates immediate associations in the customer's mind. It conjures thoughts of past experiences with similar products and services. Not naming your offer is sales suicide. It's tempting to rely on your brand name. Thinking of a stellar name is

---

5. Ries, Al and Trout, Jack (2001). Positioning: The Battle for Your Mind: The Battle for Your Mind

hard. But offering "mentorship" or "coaching" sounds lame and won't create a lasting impression.

Many entrepreneurs get bogged down in the naming process. Brainstorming leads to dozens of dreadful ideas. To avoid banging your head against the whiteboard, approach the naming process with MYCRAPS. Yes, it's another acronym. Trust me, there's a method to the madness. The acronyms in this book are a marketing lesson in themselves, but I'll leave that for another book. MYCRAPS stands for:

- Major Benefit
- Yeet the Acronyms.
- Common Words.
- Rhyming.
- Alliteration.
- Proximity.
- Separate and Stack.

Major Benefit

In case you've forgotten, you're selling outcomes, not things. The old adage is that no one wants a 1/4" drill bit; they want a 1/4" hole. You could even say that people don't want a 1/4" hole; they want to hang a family portrait in the living room. People want the result. When you build a product name around its major benefit, you grab attention.

Think back to the earlier copywriting course example. The course's length was its major benefit. In less than sixty minutes, it taught non-writers how to write sales copy. The time-crunched solopreneur will gravitate to this course for its primary benefit. A stand-out name, based on the major benefit, could be:

- 60-Minute Sales Pages
- 60-Minute Sales Copy
- One-Hour Solopreneur Sales Pages
- The 60-Minute Copywriter

By focusing on the primary sales benefit, you do much more than grab attention. A name like 60-Minute Sales Pages communicates a lot of product details. It tells prospects the course takes an hour to complete and helps them write better sales pages. It's obvious. And obvious is always better than clever. Revisit the work you did on positioning, define the major benefit, and build your name from there. I've launched several courses which have names based on the major benefit. These include:

- Algorithm Hacker Blueprint
- Copywriting for Social Media
- Canva Content Mastery
- Instagram Reels Mastery
- Email Swipe File Hub

If all you do is base your product name on its major benefit, you're halfway to success.

Yeet the Acronyms

Although I love an acronym, you'll never see one in my product and service names. This is because acronyms only work for well-established businesses and brands. Imagine if I called the Posts to Profits Process the P2P Method. The first thing prospects would ask is, *"What does P2P stand for?"* Instead of grabbing attention and starting the sales process, the name creates confusion. Unless you have a large audience that knows your brand inside-out, steer clear of acronyms. Words sell. Acronyms confuse (at least in relation to names).

Common Words

The human brain is a wonderful prediction machine. It makes constant assessments of situations and signals to influence our behaviour. Product names are no exception to the rule. Uniqueness piques our curious natural instincts, but familiarity is favourable.

Using common words is not an immutable law of naming. It's optional—a consideration. The letters S, C, P, A, and T are the most common starting letters for English words. X, Z, Y, Q, and K are the least used at the start of words. Using these in product names might seem odd in the prospect's mind. Of course, ignore this point if you're selling online training about Zoo Keeping. Zoo Keeping Made Easy is the perfect name. It's wise to favour common words if you can. But use common sense.

Rhyming

Rhymes appear everywhere: songs, slogans, brand names, and even driving guidelines. Here are several examples you might recognise.

"Only a fool breaks the two-second rule." Used on UK motorways to ensure people keep a safe distance between themselves and the car ahead.

"Beanz. Meanz. Heinz." The slogan of the world's most famous baked bean manufacturer.

"StubHub." A name that communicates a lot about the brand in a short, memorable name.

"7-Eleven." Memorable. Catchy. Simple.

"Reece's Pieces." A much better choice than 'Reece's Bits' or 'Reece's Minis'.

Now's the time to rhyme for a name that sticks in the mind, like mine. But, a word of caution. Don't force the rhyme if it doesn't work. The rhyme is a bonus. Highlighting the major benefit is still of primary importance. Never sacrifice clarity for clever. Zoo Keeping Made Easy is far better than Zoo 4 You.

Alliteration

PayPal, Coca-Cola, Costa Coffee, and Dunkin' Donuts all use alliteration. The same letter or sound appears at the start of the adjacent or connected words.

Alliteration is my go-to naming tactic after focusing on the major benefit. Starting words with the same letters gives the name a 'bounce,' like the timbre of a song. Alliteration creates catchy names that stick in your prospects' minds. Product recall matters. If what you sell is top-of-mind at the point of the buying decision, sales come easier. A simple name could give you a significant headstart over the competition.

To develop a name with alliteration, start by brainstorming associated words. Then, piece together a name that trips off the tongue and focuses on the product's major benefit. Here are three examples taken from my online courses.

- Social Media Sales Formula
- Product Launch Plan
- Canva Content Mastery

Proximity

Proximity is a word of caution within the naming process. Avoid names that are similar to existing competitor offers. It's the lazy approach to naming. And lazy doesn't stand out. The only thing that happens is you fall into the Association Abyss (spot the alliteration).

US tyre manufacturer, Goodrich, has fallen into the Association Abyss. The company took their name from its founder's surname. It's a logical decision, but one with a gigantic flaw. Goodyear is one of the leading tyre manufacturers in the world. Goodrich and Goodyear are too similar and cause confusion among consumers. This might not seem like a huge problem until you examine its impact on revenue.

Goodrich was the first manufacturer of steel-belted radial-ply tyres in the United States. But, when asked which company produced them, 56% of buyers said Goodyear. Strange, considering they didn't make them for the US market. Through lousy naming, Goodrich boosted their competitor's notoriety and market share. Now, Goodyear outsells Goodrich, 3 to 1. Ouch![6]

When product names are similar, people often don't remember who does what. But they do remember the market leader. Copying the competition often increases their market share, not yours. I wouldn't care if someone tried to promote "Posts Into Profits" or "Social Launching." The name isn't different enough to detract from my business. In fact, it would give me free sales. Then, I'd send in the lawyers.

Another consideration is that many successful businesses have terrible names. Success often comes despite a name rather than because of it. Being first to market or having a large following can mask the flaws in a product name. Don't get swayed by past product names. You could be basing your marketing around a lucky exception.

Separate and Stack

'Separate and Stack' (it's Alliteration Armageddon) applies to the components of the offer. People are busy and won't always pause to read every word you write. 'Separate and Stack' satisfies the sales page skimmers and caption speed readers. It helps you communicate

---

6. Ries, Al and Trout, Jack (2001). Positioning: The Battle for Your Mind: The Battle for Your Mind

the features and benefits of your service at a glance. It also elevates bland, generic things into enticing, sales-creating features. The process is simple and follows the MYCRAP structure I've outlined. The easiest way to show you how it works is with an example. Below is a two-column chart. The left column shows the standard feature of my Social Mavericks community. The MYCRAP version appears on my sales page and in my content in the right column.

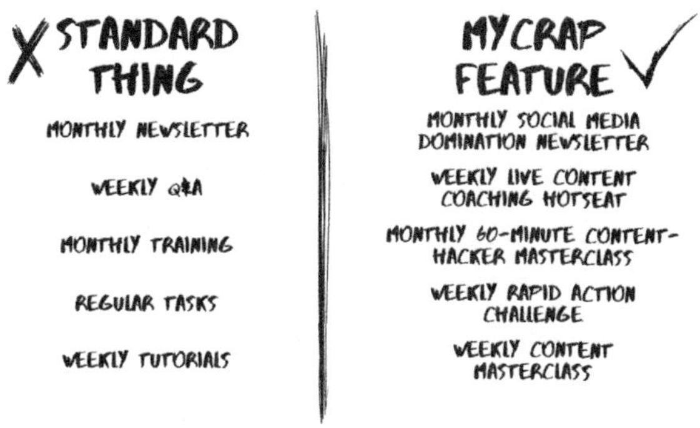

It's easy to see why the MYCRAP features lead to more sales. A simple name helps prospects understand what they're buying. It provides instant clarity. As I said at the start of the chapter, clear, simple, well-crafted, unique offers generate sales. Names matter.

Price The Thing

You could and should charge more. At least, that's my experience working with hundreds of online service businesses. But fear and averages keep many businesses poor and drive others to destruction. Business owners fear raising prices, despite inflation and rising costs. *"What if all my customers leave?"* Entrepreneurs settle for middle-of-the-road pricing because they fear losing what they have. I have a warning if you have this strange gravitation toward the market average. Soon, you'll feel undervalued and underwhelmed when the money trickles in at the end of the month. The reality is that low prices attract the most hard-to-please clients. Worse still, you'll end up resenting loyal customers and loathing your business. You'll work twice as hard for a fraction of the revenue a higher-paying client brings. And don't think generating leads will be a cinch with low pricing. The effort needed to book sales calls and sign up prospects is the same. You'll post content, create lead magnets, and drive traffic to your email list. You'll write regular emails, spend time on sales calls, and engage with your audience. Low prices don't attract easy sales. Avoid this painful future by charging what you're worth. The question is, how do you know what you're worth?

Pricing physical products is more straightforward than pricing services. Take a retail store, for example. (Note. I'm simplifying this concept because this isn't an accountancy textbook. Accountants! Look away now). You buy goods to sell in your shop. You price those goods higher than what you paid to make a profit. This is Gross Profit, i.e. the amount you earned after the basic cost of buying the goods. Net Profit is different. Net Profit takes into account all operating expenses (e.g. salary, taxes, and interest). You have a profitable business if you have a positive net profit. You can increase prices, reduce costs, or both to make your business more profitable. Play your cards right, and you can even pay yourself a dividend to buy the hot tub you've always wanted. But pricing services is not always this simple.

Delivering a service is often based on time, teaching, and communication. You're not buying widgets and selling them at a profit. My first rule of service-based pricing is to base your price on value, not time. Imagine I could guarantee to make you a million pounds in a year.

How much would you pay me? £10k? £100k? More? But what if I could guarantee to make you a million pounds in a minute? Would you pay more for faster results? Sane people would say yes. Here's another example. A business owner is getting several quotes from designers to create a new company logo. The first designer estimates designing the perfect logo will take ten hours. This designer charges £100 per hour and quotes £1,000. Then, the business owner comes to me. I'm a badass logo designer (I'm not, by the way. I'm pretending). I have over 15 years of experience working with top global brands. Over the years, I've developed a smooth process that enables me to design logos within one hour. Using the hourly rate from the first quote, would £100 be a fair price? No. Charging £100 would punish me for being exceptional at my job. I should (and would) charge more because I price my service on value, not time. Experts are faster, have more experience, and often deliver better results. All these things benefit the customer, so the price tag should reflect those benefits.

Rule Two of pricing contradicts Rule One (a bit). It's helpful to understand your hourly rate, so you know you're not working for a pittance. Imagine you charge £100 per month for 1:1 coaching. Your service involves a lot of direct communication, calls, emails, texts, and so on. On average, you spend ten hours a month delivering the service. In this scenario, you're earning £10 per hour. You could make more working at McDonald's, Starbucks, or driving for Uber. This might be ok as a short-term solution to get started, but you must be aware of what's a profit and what isn't.

Rule Three says that the mechanism should influence the price point. Your prospects will have rough expectations about how much various services will cost. For example, I guess this book cost you less than £20. Bargain. But if I put the same information in a course, I could charge £997. It would be easier for me and far less time-consuming. Not to mention more profitable. But the market expectation dictates the price. These price expectations vary by niche, so ensure you understand your market. A-list copywriter Ben Settle often sells his books for $200 (or more). But he's an exception to the rule because he has massive authority and trust with his audience. This trust allows Ben to exceed the general price expectations.

Use the image below as a guideline for setting prices. A good heuristic is the more access a client gets to you, the more they pay.

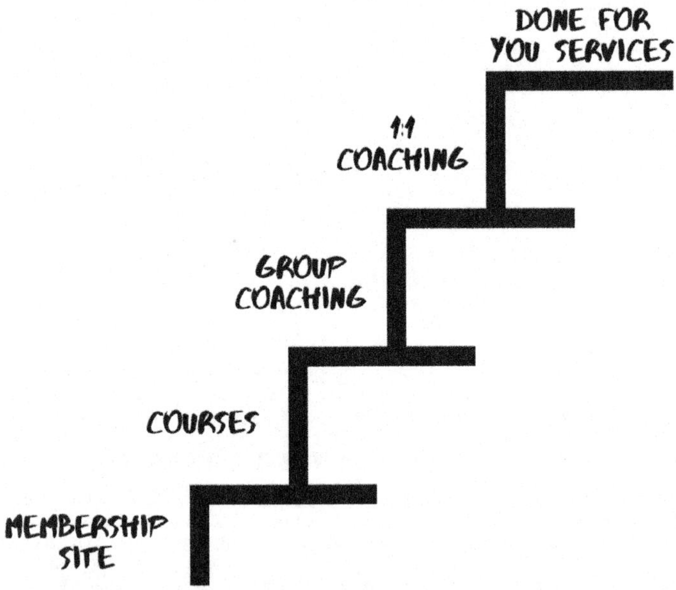

Consider Rule Four if you have authority, a unique service, or are dominating a niche. Don't use competitor pricing as your price ceiling. Don't position yourself in the middle of the pack when you have a genuine stand-out offer. It's the fastest way to devalue what you're selling. Instead, use competitor analysis to inform your decision, then consider these five guidelines.

The price of your service goes up when:

- You're the only person who can do what you do.
- You have a unique offer.
- You make success faster.
- You make success easier.
- You give the client more time and direct access.

What about if you're new in your industry? You have no authority or social proof and have minimal experience. What then? Well, if you can't tick the boxes above, you'll have to hang around in the pack until you can prove yourself. This is the time in your business when you work your butt off. Do everything possible to get the absolute best results for your clients. Because nothing says *"I'm worth more"* than a stack of undeniable proof that you get results.

Often, entrepreneurs get stuck, not knowing when to increase prices. This is where Rule Five helps. Define precise thresholds when you'll increase prices. For example, you could raise prices by £50 every time you get 20 new clients. Following a structured process means you avoid overshooting your price ceiling. Sales conversion will drop several percentage points as prices increase. Don't panic. This is normal. But keep a close eye on the relevant metrics. A small change is acceptable. Sales conversions dropping to almost zero is not.

You've defined, named, positioned, and priced your offer. Now you have to persuade people to buy it.

Sell The Thing

Marketing is manipulation, no matter how you dress it up. You're trying to persuade someone to do something. It might be in that person's best interests. It might be a profound, positive, life-changing decision. But it's still manipulation.

Persuasion is the polite marketing term for manipulation. Marketers use six persuasion principles, first identified by Robert Cialdini.[7] Almost every marketing book since the mid-80s references Cialdini's work. Cialdini is the G.O.A.T of persuasion. His seminal book *Influence: The Psychology of Persuasion* is a must-read. As is his follow-up *Pre-suasion: A Revolutionary Way to Influence and Persuade*. Here are the six persuasion principles:

- **Reciprocity.** When you give, people want to give back.
- **Commitment and Consistency.** People want to be consistent with their actions.
- **Social Proof.** Showcase other people's success.
- **Liking.** You don't buy from people you don't like.
- **Authority.** We buy from people we trust. And we trust people with authority.

---

7. Cialdini, Robert. (2007). Influence: The Psychology of Persuasion.

- **Scarcity.** *"Holy shit! There's only one copy of Posts to Profits left. I better grab it now."* You know, that type of thing.

I won't do his entire life's work a disservice by cramming everything you need to know into a couple of paragraphs. If you want the full detail (which I recommend), grab the books and read them several times.

Without realising, you've learned about several persuasion triggers in prior chapters. But there are a couple I haven't mentioned... until now.

Social Proof

Whenever you post a client update on Instagram, that's social proof. When you include a testimonial on a sales page, that's social proof. If you take screenshots of group coaching calls. If you share customer posts about your course, this is social proof.

Most prospects don't want to be trailblazers. People want to invest in what's tried and tested. You must show that others have invested in your service and are getting the results you promise. This social proof eliminates doubt in the prospect's mind.

The trick is to share social proof from customers who epitomise your ideal clients. This gets your prospects to think, *"That could be me."* You can enhance this feeling by focusing on the Universal Problem. It's a way of zeroing in on the aspect of a success story that resonates with prospective customers. You'll learn about the Universal Problem in section Part Three.

"But, Simon. Why social proof posts never get any engagement."

Social proof posts often get the least engagement but make the most sales. Let's say you post a weight loss transformation on Instagram. You can see a visible difference between the before and after images. Your ideal customer finds your profile and decides to scan through your content.

"Wow. She got phenomenal results."

* Swipes down to look at more posts.

"Jeez! What a transformation."

* Swipes down to look at more posts.

"This woman is a badass coach. How much does she charge?"

The prospect checking out your profile has no need to click on each post, like it, and reply with a comment. As the cliche goes, the picture tells a thousand words. Your social proof acts like a constant sales tool on your page. It's like sales wallpaper. If these posts didn't exist, prospects might think, *"Does this person work with real people? Are they legit?"*

Of course, there are exceptions. Some businesses, including mine, don't share client results on social media. Many customers want to keep their success private. Respect their decision, and find creative ways to showcase what you do.

Scarcity

Scarcity doesn't mean scaring. Well, it does, but hear me out. Marketers can use scarcity for good and evil. The evil approach is to use fake scarcity to pressure prospects into buying. Avoid these tactics at all costs. Don't tell your followers you have two spaces left when you'd take on another twenty if you could. Don't give people a deadline, then keep extending it because of "high demand." If, in reality, "high demand" means you haven't made enough sales, people will see through the deception.

The ethical approach you should use uses honesty to give people a reason to act now. Either tell people how their life improves by making a decision or what they'll miss out on by not making a decision. But ensure the scarcity is genuine.

There are five types of scarcity that you will use most often.

- **Limited spaces.** *"I only have 5 coaching spaces available before I hit capacity. DM me COACHING for more information and to grab your spot before it's too late."*
- **Limited amount.** *"We only printed 100 copies of our latest book. When they're gone, they're gone. We're never printing these again."*
- **Deadlines.** *"The monthly newsletter hits the printers on August 1st. You've got until midnight on July 31st to subscribe. We don't sell back issues, so if you miss it, you'll miss out."*
- **Exclusive bonuses.** *"You can grab exclusive bonuses worth over £1,000 when you buy our course before midnight on Sunday. After that, they're gone for good."*
- **Time-or-volume-sensitive pricing.** *"Because this is a new service, we are offering customers who jump on board early a MASSIVE discount. If you're one of the first 100 people to join the monthly membership, you'll get 50% off for life!"*

Some people hate scarcity and think it's sleazy. Others think it doesn't work. Both are wrong. Scarcity is only sleazy if you use it with bad intentions. And even though you think it doesn't work, it definitely, definitely does.

There are frequent occasions where typical scarcity tactics don't apply. Your company might be in its infancy and be nowhere near capacity. And you don't have specific deadlines because you always take on clients. But there are always options. Here are four to consider.

Create Moments

Chip and Dan Heath wrote a great book called *The Power of Moments*.[8] Create memorable moments that help attract new clients. You can publicly welcome new clients via a post on social media. When customers complete courses, send them certificates they can share online. And, like it or not, people love starting on Monday or waiting until the first of the month to build a new habit. Craft a relevant marketing campaign around moments on the calendar.

"Get ready for the New Year sales rush with our end-of-year marketing tune-up."

"Get record Black Friday sales with our counterintuitive email sales sequences."

"Summer shred! Get stage lean and win your pro card, then hit the Marbella beaches."

---

8. Heath, Chip and Heath, Dan. (2017). The Power of Moments: Why Certain Experiences Have Extraordinary Impact

Find moments, and use them to your advantage. The more moments you make, the stronger the pull to your service.

The Consequence of NO

Every decision you make has consequences. This includes making no decision. Some people will scour Amazon for social media marketing books and choose not to buy mine. Fools! Let's laugh at them together for their idiotic decision. Don't worry, they'll never know. Muah-ha-ha-ha-ha.

In all seriousness, there's a consequence to saying no. Not investing in your service is an active decision not to achieve that goal faster and easier. It means the person is willing to try other approaches that may have a higher probability of failure. Somewhere in your marketing, you could lean into the consequences of no.

Have an open and closed policy.

Coaching programmes and courses are often available to join 365 days a year. But this gives prospects an option to keep delaying their decision. Switching to an intake model could boost sign-ups. Don't worry. You won't miss sales closing your doors. You create scarcity and the need to buy the next time. You force people into a decision because they don't want to wait three months for the next intake. At the time of writing, my course, Social Launch, runs four times a year. I could let people join at any time, but by restricting access, each intake becomes an event—a moment. I'm not saying you should copy this approach, but it's worth considering if your evergreen method isn't working.

Onboarding capacity

I have to manage when new clients join my 1:1 Mentorship programme. Taking on more than five people at once would spike my workload and impact other areas of my business. So, I have an onboarding capacity. Even if I had ten spaces available, I would cap the number of people joining at any time. This scarcity isn't as powerful as an absolute limit on clients and a one-in-one-out policy, but it has an effect.

The "You can never leave" tactic.

I didn't know where to include this tactic. Is it scarcity? I'm unsure. But it works. Having a "no return" policy in your business can seem scary. It feels insensitive to tell customers they can never return if they cancel. But, it has clear benefits for you and the customer.

When prospects understand that cancelling means they can never return, they think twice. On the front end, they join when ready for a long-term commitment. It scares away the "I'll try it for a month and see what it's like" crowd, meaning you attract higher-quality customers. It also means customers think twice about cancelling. Another subscription service gets the chop before you. This only works when your offer is exceptional. If what you deliver is a bit 'meh', people won't care about not being able to come back. Make your service outstanding. Make it painful for someone to leave (in a nice way).

Bonuses

The right bonuses sweeten the deal for your prospects. And a well-crafted bonus stack makes investing in your service even more of a no-brainer. There are two methods for creating bonuses and six principles to maximise sales. I'll start with the two presentation methods: Separate and Stack and The Build. There's also a third option, which I call... Mega-Bonus. Well, I don't. But I thought a fancy name would make "combine the two methods" sound more appealing.

Separate and Stack

Most coaching programmes and online services consist of one core component. The core component is what delivers your ideal client their desired result. For a nutritionist, this might be a bespoke nutrition plan with fortnightly 1:1 reviews. But most nutritionists will provide a lot more. Separating these extras into bonuses gives the offer more gravitas.

Core Component: 1:1 nutrition coaching with a bespoke plan and fortnightly reviews.

Bonus 1: Access to a habit-tracking and nutrition-tracking app.

Bonus 2: Nutrition courses and educational video training.

Bonus 3: Exclusive access to a private, members-only podcast.

Bonus 4: Access to an online community and monthly live Q&A.

Bonus 5: Monthly newsletter simplifying the latest research.

Separating the components into distinct bonuses gives them tangible value. Intelligent marketers will add a monetary value to each bonus. This stacks the service and value for the prospect. Now, the service is a steal.

The Build

Use The Build if your offer is simplistic or you have several bonus options that aren't part of the core offer.

Over the years, I've accumulated dozens of training videos and resources that I use for bonuses. For example, I included several bonuses when launching my online course, Social Launch. I wanted to encourage as many people as possible to take the course. So, I built an incredible core offer and piled the bonuses high. The bonuses included:

Bonus 1: Copywriting for Social Media course (worth £299)

Bonus 2: Lead Magnet Mastery online course (worth £299)

Bonus 3: Instagram 101 online course (worth £299)

Bonus 4: Instagram Reels Mastery online course (worth £299)

Bonus 5: Ten copies of the Flight Plan newsletter (worth £490)

Bonus 6: Canva template packs for social media (worth £110)

Bonus 7: Access to the Social Mavericks Content Vault (worth £640)

The bonus build was worth over £2,300. These extras weren't part of the core offer but helped create a compelling reason to buy.

You don't need to include bonuses in your offer, but they often remove doubt from prospects' minds. A high-value bonus stack is a fantastic sales tool.

The third bonus option is to combine the two approaches. Separate the components of your offer and display them as bonuses. Then, build on this with more bonuses to seal the deal. But before you throw a bunch of worthless bonuses together, hold up. There are six principles to follow.

The Six Bonus Principles

1. **Help achieve the primary goal.** Bonuses should help the prospect achieve their desired goal faster and easier. If the bonuses don't relate to the primary goal, they will feel worthless to potential customers.

2. **Make each bonus more valuable than the main offer.** Imagine you priced your primary offer at £500. Your offer becomes incredible value if every bonus is worth more than £500.

3. **Name them.** Give your bonuses an attention-grabbing name to force people to take notice.

4. **Make the bonuses more desirable than the main offer.** Get people to think less, "That's nice," and more, "I want that more the main thing.

5. **Use a genuine price.** Now isn't the time to add a $997 price tag on every bonus. You lose credibility, and your bonuses lack impact when you over-value them.

6. **Add scarcity where possible.** Add time and quantity limits to your bonuses to increase the need to buy now. Potential customers won't want to miss out on high-value bonuses.

Use scarcity tactics to increase the urge to buy now.

Using all six principles in your bonus strategy is not always possible. But don't worry. You can still create a compelling offer by adhering to two or three principles.

Guarantees

Guarantees are a simple way to overcome objections. A well-positioned guarantee provides unsure prospects with the confidence to invest. Think of guarantees as a risk reversal mechanism. It's your opportunity to take on the risk in the buying relationship. Not only that, but it shows confidence in your ability to deliver on your promises.

Any guarantee should be as simple, bold, and long as possible. Customers get confused by a long checklist of loopholes and clauses. This could sometimes raise red flags and scare people away—the opposite of the guarantee's purpose.

Bold guarantees show that you have unbridled confidence in your service. The time frame you choose depends on the offer and the risk you're willing to take. But, if you back yourself to deliver phenomenal results, a bold guarantee is no risk at all.

There are two main types of guarantee that I recommend. Others work but are complicated or don't fit with most online service businesses.

The first guarantee is the 100% Money-Back Guarantee. It's simple, straightforward, and transparent. The customer's unhappy, they get a full refund, no questions asked. The second option is No Guarantee. This is a bold position that's often used by well-established businesses.

It's a sign of confidence and dominance. But, it might not work well if you're a relative unknown in your industry. In the early days, it may be prudent to include a bold guarantee.

There's another type of risk I recommend for high-ticked services. I call it "The Contract Get-Out." Many coaches have minimum terms, be it three months, six months, or longer. These extended commitments can cause prospects to get nervous about investing. If the service is shoddy, no one wants to be tied into a lengthy, expensive contract. So, you can ease the prospect's nervousness by including a get-out option. For example, if within the first 28 days, the customer isn't satisfied, they can opt out of the minimum term. This means that you don't have to issue a refund, which protects you for the time you invest. However, the customer isn't locked into a contract before sampling the service. There are no definitive rules about what guarantee to choose, but including one is wise.

Once you've decided on the guarantee you'll offer, name it. A well-crafted name can help your guarantee stand out on a sales page. After all, your guarantee is worthless if no one knows it exists. Iron Paradise Fitness had the Iron Clad Guarantee. Social Launch offered the "Punch a Puppy" guarantee. It's hard to know how much these guarantees influenced sales. But I guarantee (pun intended) the value of converted sales outweighs the cost of any refunds.

AN INTERLUDE...

"We interrupt this program to annoy you and make things generally irritating."

Monty Python

Part Three of the book is a couple of page-turns away. You'll discover how to create a content strategy to attract consistent leads. I know you want to move on, but first, a small request.

Right now, solopreneurs like you are struggling to grow their businesses. They're trying hard and have the desire, but they feel lost. Many will give up, resigning themselves to a life unfulfilled.

My mission is to help great online businesses escape the entrepreneurial abyss. But first, I need to reach them. This book gives entrepreneurs a low-cost way to access marketing strategies worth thousands. I'm giving away resources to make it easy to take advantage of what you learn. If you find the book valuable, how would you like to help your fellow entrepreneurs? It's simple and takes less than a minute. I can't promise it will bring you anything other than a warm, fuzzy feeling. But there's a lot to be said for helping others with zero expectations.

Here's your mission, should you choose to accept it... Take a brief moment to give an honest review of the book on Amazon. That's it. Nothing more. A rating and written review go a long way to ensure Amazon's algorithms show the book to the right people. Your words make a massive difference and mean more than you realise. Part Three will be here waiting for you when you get back. So take a break, share your thoughts, and help those who most need it.

Thanks,

Simon

Now... On with the show.

PART THREE:

THE GRAVITY METHOD

YOUR GRAVITY

HOW YOU ATTRACT
PROSPECTS TO WHAT
YOU'RE SELLING

Chapter 10

YOUR GRAVITY

The Gravity Method: Part Three

"We're caught in a tractor beam. It's pulling us in! There's got to be something you can do!"

Luke Skywalker

"There's nothing I can do about it, kid."[1]

Han Solo

Business died today. Or maybe, yesterday; I can't be sure. At least, that's how I felt at the end of 2018 when I faced the prospect of quitting. Iron Paradise Fitness was losing clients, and I couldn't replace them fast enough. I had maxed out organic opportunities and was dipping deep into my savings to stay afloat. Then, the call came. It was my business mentor.

1. Lucas, George. (1980). Star Wars: The Empire Strikes Back. Dir. Irvin Kershner.

"Hey, Simon. We're offering a new Facebook ad service." He said. I could sense the excitement in his voice. Or was it nervousness? He knew things weren't going well, so pitching me an expensive idea was risky. Regardless, he continued. *"We do everything. Plan the ad, write the script, edit the videos, and manage the campaigns. Everything."*

I was desperate. With gut-churning trepidation, I invested £3k (almost all the money I had left) for "leads on tap." But it all fell apart from day one.

My mentor promised his copywriter would script the perfect video advertisement. The expert wordsmith would mirror my brand voice and style, tailoring the right sales message for my niche. When I read the magical script, I was fuming.

My mentor sent me the script and an example video from another of his clients. The plan was to watch the clip and pay attention to how the person recorded the video. Fine, I thought. I pressed play on the video, but it wasn't the lighting, background, or energy that grabbed my attention. It was the words coming from the person's mouth. Every sentence was a carbon copy of the "bespoke" script I'd received. So much for tailoring the video to my voice and niche. After listening to me spitting fire down the phone, my mentor told the copywriter to start from scratch. With a new, though still imperfect, script in hand, we pressed forward. But the woes of paid traffic didn't end there.

Following "Scriptgate," I continued to pay the agency's fees and monthly ad spend. The ads drove traffic to a free 5-day challenge that I delivered once a month. Sign-ups were poor. Those who joined the challenge were either from the wrong niche or didn't show up for the event. After several months of haemorrhaging money, I decided to stop the bleeding. I forget how much I invested before switching off the ads. Somewhere in the region of £5k. The return on that investment? A whopping £158, which taxes and expenses reduced to £0. The leads weren't on tap. There wasn't even a trickle. I was experiencing a severe drought.

I thought it was the end. Time to close the doors on Iron Paradise Fitness. Time to head back to the daily drudge of corporate life. But there's one thing you must realise if you want any degree of success. Failure is inevitable, and you will lose money. What separates the successful from the broke is how you respond to adversity. I don't like failing, and I sure as hell don't enjoy losing money, but I don't fear it. Failure fuels my ambition. As long as I can stay above water and keep fighting, I know that, in time, I'll succeed.

Entrepreneurs crumble when they allow the fear of failure to limit their decisions. Fear of failure will cause you to miss opportunities and recoil when you should push forward. You'll be too scared to post that video that could bring you vital leads. You'll second-guess sending that marketing email that could result in several sales calls. The list of missed opportunities is endless. You will always struggle until you learn to accept setbacks as part of the process.

I was in what Seth Godin calls The Dip.[2] Faced with the prospect of closing the doors on Iron Paradise Fitness, I had one choice to make. Accept defeat and beg for my old job back, or commit to finding a way through the situation. Through dogged hard work and a willingness

---

2. Godin, Seth. (2007). The Dip: The extraordinary benefits of knowing when to quit (and when to stick).

to live like a peasant, I made it through the difficult spell. But I was still stuck in The Dip.

It was March 2019. I had switched mentors and now worked with Jordan Syatt and Mike Vacanti. Jordan and Mike were Gary Vaynerchuk's personal trainers. Both guys have successful, multi-six-figure coaching businesses. The guys achieved what I wanted, so I was eager to learn their methods. But it wasn't talk of funnels, automation, and websites that profoundly affected my future. It was one phone call.

"Yo." The text message read. It was Jordan Syatt. *"You around?"*

"Yo. Yep. Just in the gym smashing some leg curls." I replied.

"Up for a quick call? All good if you're too busy."

Of course I'm up for a call. Developing the hammies can wait. Jordan and I spoke for about twenty minutes. We discussed my business and the challenges I faced. He congratulated me for what I'd achieved thus far and for staying consistent. We discussed my frustration with not getting the likes, leads, and sales I hoped for. Like many coaches, I felt I was doing everything right, but I was deep in The Dip. I was scratching and clawing. Trying to find a way out, but it felt like I was getting nothing in return.

Jordan told me that success still takes time, even if you do everything right. Some people get lucky; they're in the right place at the right time. He told me that my struggles would be part of the epic story I would tell years from now. Because trying and failing is the fastest way to success. He was right. Four years later, I am telling you this story, which feels like a distant memory.

As we finished the call, Jordan said something that would become my mantra for years to come. I wrote it on the whiteboard above my desk as a constant reminder of my daily focus.

"Do one thing today that helps one person keep going. And do the same for yourself."

This is the reality of building a business. It's hard. The constant stresses and strains break many people. It's the resilient who make it through. I want to give you the warts-and-all truth behind my success for one simple reason. Even with this book in your hand, creating a successful online business will not be easy. It'll be easier, but never easy. The good news is that by reading this book, you'll have the rapid headstart I would have loved. You'll skip years of trial and error, heartache, and frustration.

What got me through those desperate times—The Dip—was a commitment to skill acquisition. I knew I could attract my ideal clients if I could write, design, record, and edit great content.

"Persistent people are able to visualise the idea of light at the end of the tunnel when others can't see it." - Seth Godin, The Dip.[3]

I developed systems, strategies, and processes that pulled people into my World. I had a Content Tractor Beam, which was on full-blast, 24/7. Posts, podcasts, and videos brought consistent leads even if they got mediocre engagement. My content was the Gravity that drew

3. Ibid.

people to my products and services. And now, I'm going to teach you those systems and strategies.

There are several ways to attract your ideal clients to your world. You can post organic content, run ads, delve into email marketing, promote lead magnets, or all the above.

People often think that because I focus on organic content, I think you should avoid paid advertising like the plague. Far from it. Paid adverts are a great way to boost leads in the early days of your business. Once you have an offer you know people want and a marketing process that converts leads into clients, amplifying the process with ads is a smart move. But I'll be the first to admit I'm not a paid advertising expert. So, I won't touch on social media ads in this book.

The primary focus of the Posts to Profits process is organic content, lead magnets, and email marketing. Email marketing is a huge topic and deserves its own book. I'll cover it briefly to help you understand the basics. But I'll save the detail for *Posts to Profits: Volume II: The Email Strikes Back* (if such a book will exist). With that said, let's start building your organic content strategy with my six-step process.

CHAPTER 11

THE 6-STAGE CONTENT STRATEGY

The Gravity Method: Your Gravity

"Tactics without strategy is the noise before defeat."[1]

Sun Tzu

In dreams, clients are desperate to work with you, and they engage with every post you make. But this is not a dream. It's reality.

Social media is a battle for attention. And you're not fighting with one or two close competitors. You're at war with every account related to your prospects' interests. Politics, fashion, movies, music, nutrition, lifestyle, memes, the list is endless. It's foolish to expect engagement because you spent hours editing a video. Heck! It's not only foolish; it's arrogant and smacks of entitlement. It's why the *"Show up daily"*

1. Tzu, Sun. (2010). The Art of War. CreateSpace Independent Publishing Platform

trope is never enough. You need to do more than show up—much more. Because, the truth is, no one owes you their time.

A marketing strategy is the only way to guarantee a profitable online business. The problem is most struggling entrepreneurs do nothing more than post and hope. But hope, manifestation, and clutching a clump of lucky heather as you hit 'share' is not a strategy. And if entrepreneurs aren't spraying and praying, they're at the mercy of lousy advice. Business gurus who got lucky in social media's golden age are now fonts of marketing nonsense. Back when Facebook and Instagram were novelties, creators could post anything. Reach was almost limitless because there was no competition. Fast forward a decade, and what worked then doesn't work now.

The most ludicrous advice I've ever heard was from my friend, Mal. She left me a 15-minute voicemail, updating me on her business. There was no mention of "the colours," so I knew something was wrong. She told me that she had fired her business mentor. Considering she'd invested £5k upfront and £1.5k per month after that, it was a bold decision. It's not unreasonable to expect solid advice when you're paying thousands every month. But, as you might gather, sound marketing tactics were not forthcoming.

Mal is an online fitness coach. She helps women lose weight using sustainable diet protocols and strength training. Mal lives in Dubai, where the cost of living is high. She's also a phenomenal coach with years of experience, so her prices aren't cheap. Understanding the situation, Mal's (Tor)mentor gave her the stock advice I often hear. *"Post on LinkedIn. It's where rich, busy professionals hang out."* I have nothing against LinkedIn. In fact, it's an excellent platform for finding clients if it's likely to be their platform of choice. But, almost always, business gurus trot out the advice without thinking.

"Ah. So you work with busy professionals," was this mentor's incorrect summation of Mal's business. *"Well, there's bound to be a bunch of fat people with a few quid hanging out on LinkedIn."* Hoist the red flag high. This guy is about to win Business Bullshit Bingo.

Mal wasn't an avid user of LinkedIn, so she didn't know the best strategies. She turned to her 1,500-a-month mentor for guidance. The "marketing advice" the mentor gave was unbelievable. *"Search for people with round faces and message them to see if they need to lose a few pounds."* Ladies and gentlemen, we have just lost cabin pressure. Prepare for implosion.

Terrible advice is common. Often, it's the norm. As a result, entrepreneurs have a distorted view of strategy. Creators are under the illusion that deciding whether to post a video or image is a content strategy. It is not. Neither is allocating specific topics to the days of the week, e.g. Testimonial Tuesday. These things can be part of a strategy, sure. But as standalone activities, they are nothing more than a random to-do list. And random isn't reliable.

Your marketing strategy must be a set of cohesive actions. These coordinated actions should help you solve a specific problem. In the beginning, your strategy might contain assumptions and guesswork. Don't worry. Even marketing experts with decades of experience are guessing. The only difference is their guesses are often correct. Remember that your strategy isn't set in stone. It's evolving. You can and will adjust your strategy as you learn what generates results.

There are three parts to the ideal marketing strategy. You've discovered two already—Your People and Your World. Now it's time to complete The Gravity Method with the final element—Your Gravity. Within Your Gravity is your organic content strategy, which comprises six stages: Plan, Create, Post, Interact, Generate, and Sell.

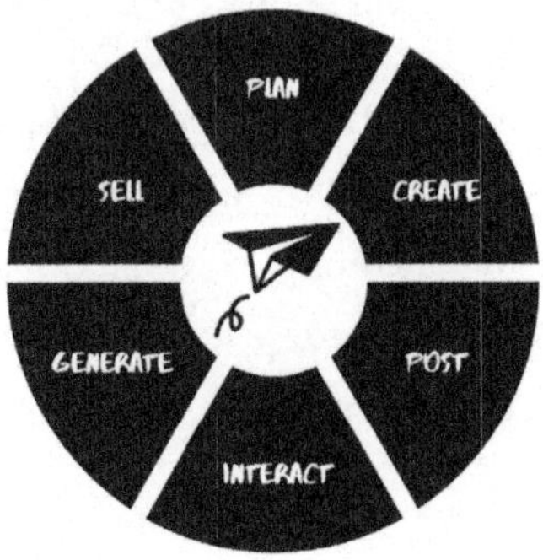

Your strategy is a list of actions that solve a specific problem. The problem I assume you face is not getting consistent leads and sales from social media. Or, you're getting consistent leads and want more. Either way, you won't solve this riddle with low-level 'post and hope' tactics. To build a profitable online business, you must think more broadly. Your new approach to content strategy starts with setting your intentions from the outset.

Set The Intention

The image on the next page depicts the highway to social media sales hell. The process looks simple. Create content, pitch an offer, and people buy. I wish it were this simple, but it isn't. At least, not for most online businesses. This approach is like propositioning a stranger for sex after a two-minute chat. You might get a yes, but the odds and chances of a long-term relationship are low. The best tales of enduring love don't start with, *"Well, we were both drunk and decided to have a bunk-up in the bogs."* And the most remarkable stories of sales success don't start, *"Well, I kept repeating... 'Buy my shit' every day until they caved in."* Pushing for sales with this aggressive approach comes across as needy. Read Jim Camp's *Start With No*,[2] and you'll see why neediness is the biggest mistake in any negotiation. And since sales are like negotiation, it's best to avoid neediness at all costs.

Most social media users don't swipe through their news feeds looking for something to buy. People use social media to entertain, educate, and message their friends. I don't know about you, but I don't go on a social media app and think, *"What do the 50 businesses I follow want to sell me today?"* I'm more likely to be on the hunt for memes and guitar tutorials. But even though I don't go on social media to buy, it doesn't mean I won't.

There's a crucial distinction between intent and actual behaviour. When entrepreneurs understand this difference, they create content to align with people's intentions.

Replace blunt sales pitches that feel like unwanted intrusions with value-driven content.

---

2. Camp, Jim. (2002). Start With No: The Negotiating Tools That the Pros Don't Want You to Know

Be a fisherman, not a hunter

There are two ways to get customers on social media: 'Stalk and Snare' or 'Lure and Land.' The direct pitch in the image above is the 'Stalk and Snare' approach. These marketers act like hunters. They stalk their prey, waiting for the right moment to pounce. But the hunter's prey is wary and made anxious by the hunter's tactics. One false move and the hunter goes from 'Stalk and Snare' to 'Stalk and Scare.'

Savvy marketers opt for the fishing approach. The fisher chooses to entice, attracting fish with bait. This approach takes patience. The fisher puts thought into techniques of attraction. (Unlike your ideal customers, the fish aren't willing actors in the process. But don't sweat the details. You get the point).

Many business owners hunt new customers like my half-blind Aunt, wielding an AK-47. But the better option is to attract. Be like the fisher, and let potential customers come to you. To be clear, you're not trying to lure customers with false promises. Nor are you using bait-and-switch tactics to make fast sales. The principle is that you entice prospects with a valuable offer to sell them a more beneficial offer. The image below shows the simple process flow.

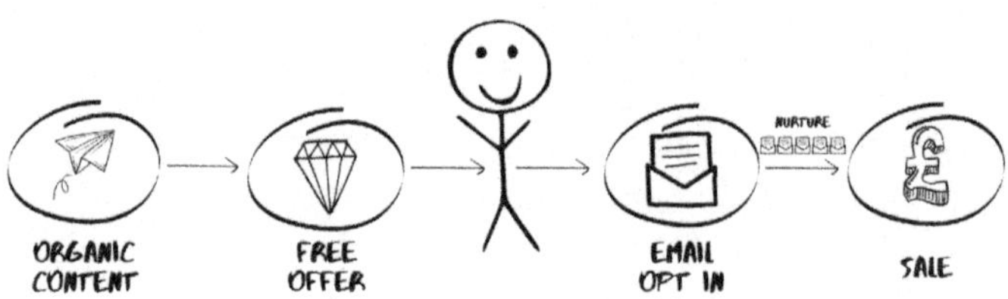

This process creates an "I want to buy your stuff" relationship. The customer is opting into the sales process. You're not railroading them into buying. You're selling to those who raise their hand and give you permission to tell them about your offers.

There are several ways to approach this kind of sales funnel. The lead magnet you choose will determine the set-up of your funnel. The image below shows you how the permission-based process works for a free webinar.

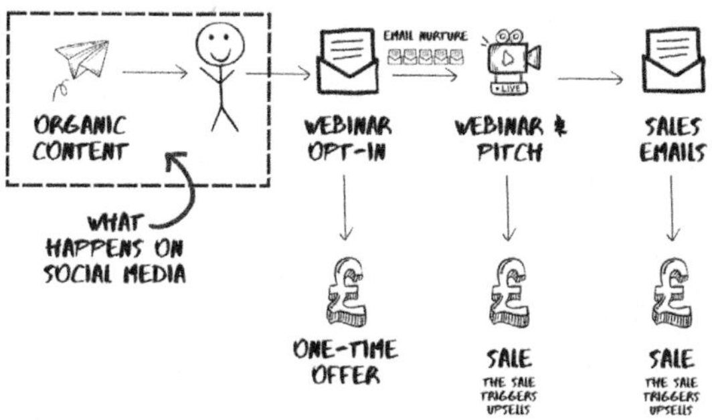

The picture below shows a variation of the process for a scorecard funnel.

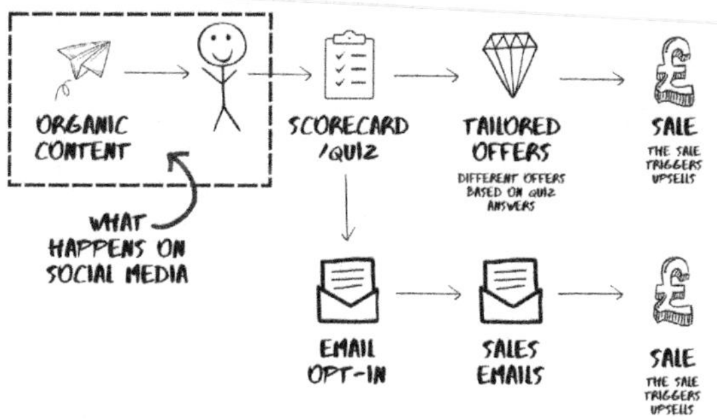

The vital thing to note is the amount of activity taking place on social media. Social media starts the process. It's the mechanism used to identify genuine prospects. Then, the back-end systems nurture these warm leads to a sale. This is what Seth Godin calls "Permission Mark eting."[3] I've embedded Permission Marketing at the heart of the Posts to Profits process. I only want to send marketing messages to people who want them. I don't waste precious time hunting and chasing. Chasing is not only needy; it erodes trust and authority. Think about the daily messages you receive from people trying to sell you stuff. Are they the world's top marketers and brands? No. The only people hammering cold DM tactics are those without an ounce of credibility. Don't position your brand in this category with thoughtless, unwanted sales tactics.

Social media is the beginning, not the end

I want you to consider social media as part of a more extensive marketing ecosystem. It's where you generate leads and start the marketing process. Use content to engage and nurture your audience. Communicate your unique thoughts, values, and methods. Provide insights and tips that solve problems. Post content filled with personality, humour, and opinions. Do all this for long enough, and you'll build trust and authority with your audience. Combine this strong customer relationship with persuasive offers, and you will get leads. All this begs the question... If you're not selling on social media, where do you sell? Enter email marketing. Because, contrary to popular belief, email isn't dead—far from it.

---

3. Godin, Seth. (2007). Permission Marketing: Turning Strangers into Friends and Friends into Customers

Social media platforms dictate which followers see your content and when. Raving fans will turn on post notifications and wait for your next post with bated breath. But these fans are the minority. The majority of your followers are too busy to care about you. Plot twist! You and your business are not the centre of everyone else's world. Shocking, I know. Your followers will engage with an intriguing post when they see one, but they're not seeking you out. This means that the algorithms control deliverability—a marketer's nightmare. Look at the statistics.

I analysed the reach rate of my content on Instagram from July 2022 to July 2023. (Reach rate is the average reach of your feed posts compared to your total following). My reach rate was 16%, which means 2,666 of my 16,668 followers saw my content. This doesn't consider non-followers, and that reach doesn't represent views. You might think 16% is low—pitiful, almost. You would be correct, but 16% is still 4% above the average for accounts of my size.

Imagine you're launching a new service. You create posts detailing the service, how it works, and why people should buy. But the algorithm destroys the process. Instead of seeing one clear, cohesive message, your marketing becomes disjointed. Users see one video here and a post there. It's out of sequence and confusing. This lack of reliable delivery is why I rarely use social media for direct sales.

Email gives marketers greater control over their communication. Typical email deliverability is c. 99%—a stark difference from social media's woeful reach. With increased deliverability, well-written emails speed up the sales process. You can build stronger, deeper connections with your audience and even pitch daily.

This doesn't mean you should never sell on social media. But there's a better approach. You don't have to send fifty cold DMs daily and ram your offer down everyone's throats to make money. I don't want a business like that. You don't want a business like that. And your audience doesn't want you to sell to them like that.

Side note. Some people will tell you that cold DMs work, i.e. they've messaged people out of the blue and made sales. The same people will tell you that selling in every post puts cash in the bank. Sure, you can make sales with these tactics, but at what cost? You won't stay in business long if you have a reputation for spamming your audience. This approach is akin to being a door-to-door salesman. You're rap, rap, rapping on the virtual doors of strangers. Those strangers don't want to buy; they want to ignore you and hope you disappear. I prefer to sell to people who raise their hand and say, *"I'm interested in what you're selling. Tell me more."*

So, the first step of your content strategy is to distinguish between your intentions. Social media is for lead generation. Email is for sales. There is room for overlap. It's not a hard delineation. However, each platform has a primary purpose.

Chapter 12

STAGE 1: PLAN

The Six-Stage Content Strategy

> "Our goals can only be reached through the vehicle of a plan. There is no other way."
>
> Pablo Picasso

Business coaches say consistency is the secret to social media success. *"Show up and give value"* is the typical trite sound bite. Not only is this advice meaningless, but it's also incomplete. Showing up is not enough. Giving value is not enough. It's vacuous advice that's like telling an obese person to *"move more and eat less."* It's TBU information: True But Useless. An obese person knows that if they ate one cheeseburger instead of ten, they might lose a few pounds. But knowledge is often not the problem. It's the myriad factors that influence daily behaviour and decision-making.

Getting leads from social media is no different. You don't need me to tell you to post more than once a week. And you already know that those posts should be valuable to your audience. The most common reason for a lack of consistency on social media is simple. Content creators don't know what to post to attract the right people and generate leads. So, when the results never come, they give up. Let's face it. If you knew almost every post you made generated leads, you'd find a way to be consistent. *"I haven't got time"* would never be an excuse. You'd find time because you view posting content as directly influencing revenue. In simple terms, consistency must produce the desired output. If it doesn't, you'll become inconsistent.

Achieving the desired output—leads—requires three things. Consistent content relevant to the target audience, combined with compelling offers. We covered the last two elements in previous chapters. And I'll guide you through lead magnets (free offers) soon. But first, Consistent, relevant content is our priority.

Consistency without relevancy is a pointless tick-box exercise. You're posting content for the sake of it, not specific, measurable outcomes. Posting daily is a waste of time if your ideal clients can't relate to your message. It's crucial to combine consistency with relevancy.

Consistency is a simple concept, so I won't waste much time explaining it. Commit to posting content as often as possible; daily is ideal. That's it. The trickier part of the equation is relevancy.

To make relevant content, you must understand your audience's wants and needs. Remember The Problem Path from the chapter on niching? Well, you're going to turn The Problem Path into a simple, effective content strategy. The aim is to build a content strategy based on giving solutions to your audience's problems.

Your Problem Path comprises three elements.

1. Starting point. What's your ideal client's current situation? What have they tried before? How do they feel about themselves and their chances of success? You won't be able to know these things for sure, but empathise as best you can.

2. Endpoint. Fast forward 12-18 months when your ideal client has achieved their goals. What is life like for them now? What does "good" look like? Have a clear definition of success.

3. Problems. What specific issues prevent your ideal client from achieving their desired goal? Do they lack time, knowledge, or confidence? Do they suffer from anxiety, limiting beliefs, or stress? Why do they need you?

The fourth step in the Problem Path process is the foundation of your content strategy.

4. Problem categories. After you've got a laundry list of challenges, group them into no more than seven broad categories. For example, mine are:

- Leads
- Instagram
- Content Creation
- Mindset
- Marketing
- Sales
- Copywriting

At this point, you could map your seven topics to the seven days of the week. This isn't terrible if predictability and structure help you stay consistent. Here's what my posting strategy would be like following this approach.

- Monday - Leads
- Tuesday - Instagram
- Wednesday - Content Creation
- Thursday - Mindset
- Friday - Marketing
- Saturday - Sales
- Sunday - Copywriting

You'll cycle through the topics quicker if you have fewer than seven categories.

- Monday - Leads
- Tuesday - Content Creation
- Wednesday - Marketing
- Thursday - Copywriting
- Friday - Leads
- Saturday - Content Creation
- Sunday - Marketing

With this approach, you're hitting every audience pain point every week. And when every piece of content resonates with your audience, they keep coming back. Soon enough, those most addicted to your content turn into red-hot leads. But we're not done yet. We want to tailor your content to match your desired market position. I'll continue using my content topics to explain.

My ideal customers have wide-ranging problems. Everything from designing infographics to writing engaging emails. I create content covering all these things but aim to carve out a specific position in my niche. I want followers to think of me as the guy who gets leads with simplified marketing strategies. But I can only signal this intent. I can't control it. So, I signal my market position by biasing my content output towards Leads and Marketing.

- Monday - Leads
- Tuesday - Marketing
- Wednesday - Content Creation or Instagram
- Thursday - Leads
- Friday - Marketing
- Saturday - Sales or Mindset
- Sunday - Copywriting

This shift would make Leads and Marketing almost 60% of my posting strategy. It's a robust and subconscious signal of my market position. Apply the same principle to your content to establish a stronger position in your niche. If you're an online fitness coach, don't post three recipe ideas every week if you want to be the "Biomechanics PT." Likewise, if you're an email marketer, don't fill your feed with Instagram sales strategies. Posting content is marketing. It's not a tick-box exercise. The goal is not to post content for the sake of it but to attract the right people.

Never lose sight of the universal problem

As the great detective Columbo always said, *"Oh... Just one more thing."* Every piece of content you create should relate to a problem from The Problem Path. This rule applies whether you're giving life updates or sharing client wins.

Social media users are selfish. People make a snap judgement about whether your post is worth their time. If your content focuses on a problem with which they identify, you have a better chance of them engaging. The mistake comes when you abandon The Problem Path. Client success posts are the perfect example. Business coaches will drill the benefits of social proof into your head. Showcasing client wins is the vital proof that you can deliver results. The more evidence of your success, the more prospects trust you with their money. Without question, social proof aids the marketing process. But standard testimonials often feel like stock, ill-conceived, and subtle-as-a-brick sales pitches. Remember, people are selfish on social media. Prospects don't care about Steve, Dave, Sandra, and Debbie. Steve made a ton of money, lost weight, and turned his life around. Good for him. But, so what? Your potential clients are thinking, *"Can you do this for me?"* This is the only question your success post should answer. This is why your content should revolve around the Universal Problem.

The Universal Problem is the primary issue you solved that made the transformation possible. Did Steve make thousands and lose weight because you destroyed his limiting beliefs? Or did you find unique ways to build habits that improved his consistency?

Honing in on the moment of change is what resonates with prospects. It instills the belief that you can help them overcome the same problem.

The Universal Problem taps into centuries-old storytelling patterns. Classic movies are the perfect example. Filmmakers craft entire stories around a moment of change. It's what award-winning storyteller Matthew Dick calls the *"Five-Second Moment."*

"All great stories—regardless of length or depth or tone —tell the story of a five-second moment in a person's life."[1]

People consider Jurassic Park a box office hit because of its ground-breaking visuals. But impressive CGI counts for nothing without a compelling story. You'll know what I mean if you've seen *Star Wars: The Phantom Menace.* Jurassic Park isn't about dinosaurs. Well, it is, but it's not the crux of the story. Movie-goers can't resonate with Velociraptors hunting their prey in a kitchen. The human story stops the movie from becoming a forgettable montage of action scenes.

Sam Neill plays Alan Grant, a palaeontologist married to Laura Dern's character, Ellie Sattler. The two are a couple, though unmarried.

---

1. Dicks, Matthew. (2018). Storyworthy: Engage, Teach, Persuade, and Change Your Life through the Power of Storytelling. Pg. 99

Grant hates kids. He considers them smelly, boring, and a nuisance, much to the dismay of Sattler.

As the movie unfolds, Grant becomes the protector of two young children. Tim, the wild-eyed, fearless young adventurer. And Lex, the old soul, wise beyond her years. Grant takes risks to protect the children and develops a deep affection for them both. In the process, he changes his mind about the little urchins being smelly and annoying. The five-second moment comes when Grant, Tim, and Lex are sitting in a tree, preparing to sleep. Grant takes a Velociraptor claw from his pocket that he's been holding on to since the previous day. He looks at the claw, thinking a million thoughts, staring at something that used to be so priceless.

When Tim and Lex start to fall asleep, Grant lets the claw fall to the ground in favour of protecting the children. Grant is letting go of old beliefs—things he once held dear. He has evolved.

This is Grant's moment of transformation. It's the end of the movie. The story is complete and only continues because there are several loose ends to tie up.

Grant has genuine affection for these children. It stands to reason that he could love others—his own. This allows Grant and Sattler to skip into the sunset and live happily ever after.

Indiana Jones And The Last Crusade is another example. The film isn't about a man trying to find the Holy Grail before the baddies get their hands on it. It's about a man of science who lacks faith. A man who, in his most desperate moment—when he must step into the abyss—finds faith when he needs to save his father.

You will find these five-second moments embedded within any great story. Knowing this vital storytelling secret is a blessing and a curse. On the one hand, you'll write better client stories focused on the Universal Problem. But you can predict how 80% of movies will end within the first ten minutes.

Before putting your finger on the keyboard, define the Universal Problem and the five-second moment. Think about the core problem you helped solve. It's important to remember that you're not making content for the clients you already have. It's for the potential clients you're trying to convert. Show people you have a solution to the issues keeping success out of reach. Whatever topic you post about, relate it to a universal problem.

The One-Page Strategy and the Midwit Bell Curve

While writing this book, I travelled to New Jersey to meet my business mentor, Chris Orzechowski. We ended up chatting about marketing strategies for seven hours straight. During the conversation, one word kept cropping up—simplicity.

Chris was going through a complete business overhaul. In 2022, his company achieved $997,000 in top-line revenue. Despite his obvious success, Chris knew complexity was curtailing growth. So, he made drastic changes. Chris stripped everything back to focus on one offer—his monthly print newsletter. Chris then listed everything he could every day, week, and month to increase sales for his primary offer. Instead of disparate focus and trying to grow several income streams, he grew one—rapidly.

My business wasn't turning over close to $1 million, but I had the same problem. And, if I didn't address it now, my hard work, dedication, and drive would stifle growth.

When I had one lead magnet and one offer, sales came without confusion. But, to grow the business, I went broader instead of deeper. I introduced new courses, a newsletter, a community, and dozens of lead magnets. But this approach did more harm than good. Multiple front-end offers confused my prospects. People often asked the difference between the offers and which they should choose. And having dozens of lead magnets attracted freebie-seekers. The worst part... I was attracting the wrong customers. People subscribed to my monthly newsletter without having any foundations in place. I was writing about the latest insights from the bleeding edge of social media marketing. These strategies were useless for people who weren't even posting content. As a result, churn was high.

It was my fault. I knew my avatar inside out and that they struggled with getting leads. The newsletter was a fantastic offer, but I was selling it to the wrong audience. Before contemplating the advanced strategies inside the newsletter, prospects needed the basics. The newsletter would make sense only with a foundation in the Posts to Profits process. I knew I had to simplify my business. I knew I had to take back control of the customer journey, delivering the right offer at the right time. Now, I have one front-end offer—Social Launch.

In trying to grow the business, I had broken my own rules of marketing. It's proof we're all human, and that building a business isn't about constant success. Failure is part of the job.

Chris and I were both victims of the Midwit Bell Curve. Most businesses start simple. You don't have a broad product range and an army of employees. It's you and your service. You're at the left side of the Midwit Bell Curve. You don't know much about growing a business, so you keep everything simple because you have no choice. As you achieve success, you drift towards the peak of the Midwit Bell Curve.

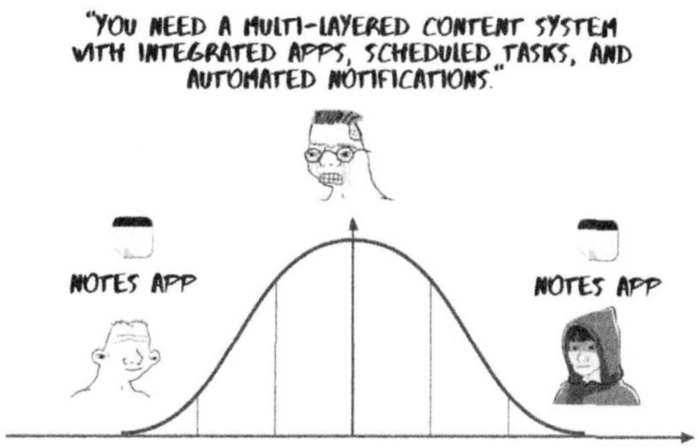

With just enough experience to be dangerous, you add more complexity. You invest in more software. You hire external agencies to manage call booking, email marketing, and social media. Before you know it, you've made a beast you can't tame. In a moment of clarity, you strip out the unnecessary crap and decide to keep things simple. You're almost back to where you started—on the other side of the Midwit Bell Curve. The Midwit Bellcurve teaches you that simplicity is almost always the better choice. It's no different with your strategy.

I've used many methods to plan content. I even developed a complex, multi-layered planning document (otherwise known as a convoluted spreadsheet with myriad tabs). I kept it up to date for about a month before realising it was taking longer to update the spreadsheet than to do the work. It was like being back in corporate business. I had flashbacks to the days spent creating presentations about our plans.

There was so much reporting we forgot to put any of the projects into action. We were like corporate dung beetles pushing bullshit around a desk.

I will save you the pain of the Midwit Bellcurve and tell you that all you need is a One-Page Content Strategy. It's not fancy, but that's the point. And it's only going to take five sentences to explain it.

Open a note-taking App on your smartphone. Ensure it's an app that's available on your phone and computer. You'll want to have easy access at all times.

Create a new note with headings for all your Problem Path topics. Add a bullet point under the relevant title whenever you have a content idea.

See... that wasn't too hard. But you wouldn't believe me if I didn't explain the need for simplicity. You'd think a complex spreadsheet is why you're not getting leads. Perverse logic would make you believe that complexity makes everything easier. It won't. Trust me. You'll be more consistent when your processes are more straightforward. But, if you want to test my theory, be my guest. I'll see you on the other side of the Midwit Bell Curve.

Finding Content Ideas

An empty note on your phone isn't groundbreaking. It's a stretch even to call it the seed of a plan, so you'll need to cram it full of ideas... fast. But how? Dreaming up new content ideas that grab attention with a vice-like grip isn't easy. It's often difficult to tell the difference between an idea that'll go viral and one that will die instantly. And even when you make what you think is the perfect post, the algorithms slam the virtual door in your face. *"Sorry. Not today. We don't need helpful content this week. Please post a video with some dance moves."*

The solution is more straightforward than you think. The first step is to abandon the desire for more likes, views, and followers. You are a marketer. You might consider yourself a creator, influencer, coach, consultant, or entrepreneur. But if you're trying to sell stuff online, you are a marketer. Allowing non-marketing metrics like followers and views to dictate marketing decisions is madness. Don't get me wrong. Social media metrics have their place. But unless you can turn engagement into cash, you're only ever trading in the currency of status.

The benefit of the Posts to Profits process is that you can create content to attract paying clients even if the algorithms hate you. The easiest place to find content ideas that generate leads is your customer base.

The people paying you money—your clients—are, by definition, your ideal customers. (Unless you've made a terrible decision to work with anyone who'll pay, of course).

Every interaction with your clients is an opportunity to generate niche-specific content ideas. It's the perfect source of creativity to help you clone your ideal clients.

Check-ins, coaching calls, community questions... Clients are telling you their biggest struggles every week. These challenges are the same problems facing your future customers. Plus, your clients will use words and phrases that resonate with your audience. This saves you time trying to find the "voice of your niche." So, add an entry to your one-page content strategy whenever you have a teaching moment with a client. Give clients a detailed answer with all the nuance needed for their circumstances. Then, give social media a slimmed-down, short, sharp summary. I aim to generate at least one content idea from every client coaching call. In reality, I have dozens.

Most of the time, I have no need to search for other ideas. But if you don't have any clients or need more inspiration, here are several suggestions.

Content For Life

At the end of each day, before shutting down your computer, take five minutes to think of at least one content idea. Note down something that happened that day that would make valuable content. This helps to train your brain to look for content ideas. I'm not a fan of setting aside a specific time to ideate. It's the fastest way to stare at a blank page and feel like a failure. Instead, keep the idea cogs turning in your brain daily. You'll find that you're never short of ideas.

Podcasts, YouTube Videos, and Articles

Other content creators who have larger audiences are an excellent source of inspiration. You're not seeking to copy their content; this is research.

Search any podcast platform for topics relevant to your niche. Take a look at the episode titles at the top of the list. Can you turn these ideas into short-form content for your social media channels? Repeat the process on YouTube and Google, and you'll have dozens of content ideas within a few minutes. But, but but... Don't copy the actual content. In fact, don't listen to the podcast, watch the video, or read the article. You don't want other creators to influence your specific ideas. The goal is to be unique.

Scan For Trends

Savvy marketers pay attention. Hop on to social media, and find a content creator in your niche with your desired audience. Then, do two things to find the best content ideas.

One, scan their profile and identify content topics that appear popular. You can't see anything except likes and views, so the posts might not generate leads. But you don't have much else to go on, so it's okay for now. You can run tests with your audience to determine which topics generate leads and which don't.

Second, if the creator often publicly responds to audience questions, take note. You're not interested in the answer. It's an irrelevant distraction. Look at the questions and how people phrase them. The questions, words, and phrases are phenomenal content fodder.

Third. Use Google Trends (type it into Google). Google Trends allows you to search keyword phrases for trending and hot topics. It's a simple way to tap into the issues your ideal clients search for on Google.

Ask Your Audience

It seems obvious, but most entrepreneurs don't do it. If you want to know what content your audience will love, ask them. Send your email list a short survey asking what they struggle with the most. You can run polls, host lives, and answer audience questions on social media.

Often, the best content ideas don't come from sitting at your desk but from your audience.

Forums, Groups, and Question Sites

Head over to where your audience hangs out and discusses their challenges. Join Facebook groups and Reddit threads to discover common pain points and offer help. The closer you get to your ideal client, the better your ideas. There is no excuse for being bereft of content ideas. Considering all the options available, it's easier to have ideas than not. And don't worry about feeling like you're saying the same thing over and over again. Repetition in marketing is necessary. Imagine if Nike said, *"Just Do It"* once. Would it stick in the minds of millions? No. The same goes for your marketing messages. Repetition is necessary if you want people to think like you and warm to your values. Just try to approach the same topic from different angles.

Try New Ideas

When I was a teenager in the mid-90s, I was obsessed with Metallica. I used to watch the documentary, *'A Year And A Half In The Life Of...'* several times every few months. I knew it word-for-word. In the first part of the film, there's a scene where James Hetfield is tracking vocals for the Black Album. He's alone in the vocal booth with Bob Rock, his producer, on the other side of the glass. Hetfield is known for his iconic screams of "Yeah" in almost every song (multiple times). During the vocal session, Bob Rock challenges Hetfield to do something different. He says, *"Let's don't do a Yeah. Do something else."* His genius suggestion is... *"Woman. Fire woman."*

It doesn't work. It's a terrible idea. But, they weren't afraid to try something off the wall to ensure the best ideas made it onto the record. Do the same. Don't add "Firewoman" to the end of every video. But, experiment with ideas.

Aerosmith was another band willing to try new ideas. The famous rockers had a weekly ritual where they would each present a terrible idea. Nine times out of ten, the ideas were shit. But one in ten was absolute rock 'n' roll gold. *'Dude looks like a lady.' 'Love in an elevator.'* These songs helped make Aerosmith a household name, and they were all born from these sessions where they dared to suck.

It's easy to shy away from new ideas when you're unsure of the outcome. Sensing impending embarrassment if you fail again, you clam up and always play it safe. But safe, generic content doesn't stand out and leaves you feeling stuck.

The truth is, you'll never be sure of the outcome. It's rare that life gifts you success on a silver platter. You have to take the risk. It's like expecting to become the Heavyweight Champion without getting punched in the face. If you're going to win the fight, you have to get in the ring. You will take punches to the face. You might even lose a few fights. But champions try, and winners dare to suck. Because when you suck—which is inevitable—you learn. You gain experience and knowledge you'll never get as a ringside spectator.

You might not be stepping into a boxing ring, but you have your battleground. You have to be willing to step through the ropes and face your challenges with no guarantee of the outcome. If you second-guess and overthink your decisions, you deny yourself the joys you seek. At some point, you have to try. You have to take a risk.

Deciding How to Share Your Message

There's no formula to decide what content format to communicate your message. Formats come and go, and their primary purpose changes in line with user behaviour. But two principles should influence your decision: audience and outcome. Before creating your next post, ask yourself three questions. For whom are you making the content? What format would best help the user retain and use the information? And, what outcome do you want for the user and yourself? Answer these questions, and choosing the most suitable format is a cinch.

Chapter 13

STAGE 2: CREATE

The Six-Stage Content Strategy

"...you've got to keep them from falling asleep."[1]

Philip Yordan

I'm the laziest hard-working hustler you will ever meet. I work hard. I'm committed to my business and my clients. But I don't want to work more than necessary to get the best results.

It makes sense. Who would work themselves into the ground if they could get the same results with half the work? No one. I've developed my businesses and the Posts to Profits method on this same premise. My drive to be lazy has led to creative ways to approach content creation. I can now post across multiple platforms with no video editors, marketing team, or VA.

My secret? Hero content. It's a process that will save you time and stress and keep you more consistent than ever.

1. McGilligan, Patrick. (1997). Backstory 2: Interviews With Screenwriters of the 1940's & 1950's

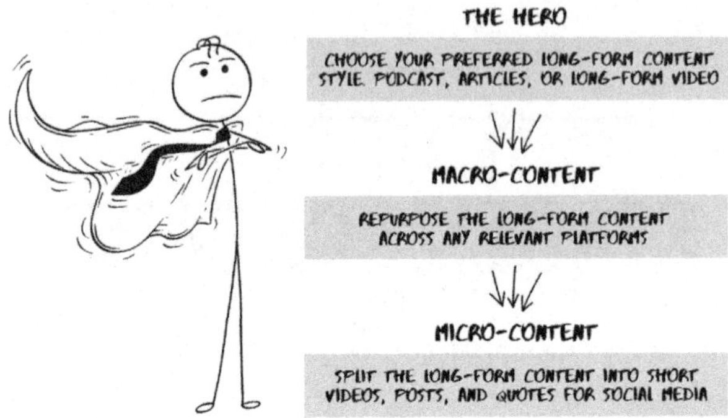

The process starts with the Hero. This is long-form content that taps into your zone of genius. There are four options: articles, podcasts, long-form videos, and live streams. For example, if you love writing, choose articles. But if you hate writing and love delivering knowledge in a live setting, pick live streams. There is no right or wrong. Choose the option you enjoy most. Your aim is to create a piece of hero content every week. You can make more, but start with one, get confident with the process, and build from there.

The primary benefit of starting with long-form content is longevity. Social media content has a short shelf life. Once a post is over a few months old, the algorithms rarely display it to users. And even your raving fans won't scroll through years of content, hoping to find a post that might not exist. Conversely, Google indexes articles, podcasts, and YouTube videos. Long after you hit publish, Google shows your content to thousands of prospects. You don't have to lift a finger. For example, an Article I wrote in January 2019 is still in the top five of Google, more than four years after I published it. Despite the fact the business no longer exists, I still get hits on the CTAs embedded in the article. Creators narrowly focused on social media miss this huge lead generation opportunity. So don't sleep on the world's largest search engine. It's still a phenomenal source of leads.

Once you've chosen your Hero, you'll create macro content. This is optional, but at least consider it. The process is simple. Take your Hero content and repurpose it across any relevant platforms. For example, you can read an article aloud and publish it as a podcast. You could simultaneously record a video of you reading through the article. This would be a simple way to create consistent YouTube content. It's minimal effort with massive benefits when you consider discoverability and longevity. Likewise, you can use transcription services to turn podcasts and videos into articles. You can crank your content machine hard with minimal effort and start churning out leads.

The third and final stage of Hero Content is Micro Content. In this stage, you create summaries, short clips, and quotes from your Hero content. Well-structured long-form content can often turn into dozens of social media posts. You can then distribute this across all relevant platforms.

When you have the Hero Content process in place, staying consistent is easier than you think.

Three Things You Need For Great Content

One thing that stops entrepreneurs from achieving their full potential is procrastination. And there's no worse time-wasting activity than fussing over equipment and software.

Having posted and analysed thousands of videos and images on social media, I can confidently tell you... Professional lighting, microphones, and cameras will never rescue lousy content. As I've said, the message is more important than the mechanism. A terrible idea won't go viral because you filmed it with a posh mirrorless camera. Think of it like *Star Wars Episode I: The Phantom Menace*. The movie was stunning. The visuals were ahead of their time, unlike anything movie-goers had seen. But the film sucked. To this day, Star Wars fans still prefer the original low-budget movies from the '70s and '80s. So, don't lose sight of what matters. Don't let equipment and software stop you from posting content.

There are only three things you need to create content.

1. A smartphone.

2. 20 seconds.

3. A good idea.

Point your phone at your face and talk. Write a helpful tip or insight in your Notes app, take a screenshot, and post it. If what you share resonates with your audience, you have a quality post. And that post will help you generate leads in the future. Worry about making your content fancy later. Communicate your unique message. Needless distractions obstruct consistency and delay success.

Three Rules of Niche Content

I've completed hundreds of social media account audits. I've reviewed accounts with fewer than 1,000 followers and some with nearly 1,000,000. It's given me unique insights into why people struggle to connect with their audience. Successful accounts have one thing in common: their content is niche-focused. Flick through their most recent posts, and you can tell what they do and whom they help. You don't have to read their bio, click links, and scroll through sales pages. It's clear within seconds. Conversely, those struggling to connect with their audience post generic and forgettable content. It's so generic it could apply to any man, woman, or Greater Spotted Eagle. Niching is non-existent.

Look at your last nine posts on your primary platform. Now answer this question. *"How many posts could apply to any niche other than the one you're trying to serve?"* For example, have you created a video entitled *"How to create a calorie deficit"*? It could be a valuable piece of content. But there's nothing about the post that applies to an identifiable niche.

Too many posts like this turn your social media account into an easily skipped profile. And that's the death knell for leads and clients.

How can you tweak your content to make it relevant to your niche? Let's use the *"How to create a calorie deficit"* post as an example. Here are several headline changes you could make for a specific niche.

For Busy Moms. *"Simple diet solutions for Moms on the go."*

For Vegan Bankers. *"Vegan weight loss solutions if you work 10 hours a day."*

For Retired Athletes. *"Fat loss solutions to regain your athletic body."*

With a few simple changes, I've made the content niche-focused. Take the principle a step further by incorporating niche wording and references. For example, you could start the video by saying, *"If you're a*

Mom who struggles to lose weight, listen up. The reality is this... young children are unpredictable. They don't stick to routines, so it's hard to plan workouts and consistently eat healthy food. Here are 3 tips to help you lose weight with minimal effort..."

You're sorely mistaken if you think niching stops at what you write in your profile. Niching applies to your content, words, references, values, opinions, and coaching ethos. To connect with your audience, approach content creation from their perspective, not yours. The difference is MASSIVE!

Creating niche-specific content is crucial for attracting your ideal customers. Your audience must feel like your content is for them. Every post, video, and story must relate to their circumstances and challenges. Content that could apply to anyone appeals to no one. Even the most factual, practical information dies if you don't make your audience care. The question is, how? How do you make niche-specific content when the topics could apply to anyone? I'll revert back to the calorie deficit example to explain.

A calorie deficit is the most (but not the only) important factor for fat loss. It's a universal truth whether you're a man, woman, busy professional, working Mum, vegan, or carnivore. (Don't email me if you disagree. I don't care). But there's always an angle—an approach to a generic topic that helps bring it to life for your niche. The process starts with three rules of niche content.

Rule #1: How does the topic fit into their life?

Your audience won't remember a list of facts. They're not Rain (Wo)Man. Use relevant stories instead of pounding people's feeds with fact after fact. Stories are a fantastic way to ensure your message sticks in your followers' minds.

"But what's a relevant story, Simon."

I don't mean you should record a 15-second version of The Empire Strikes Back. Place the topic within the daily life of your ideal customer. Imagine your perfect customer is a stressed-out stay-at-home Mum. Instead of regurgitating the facts of a calorie deficit, make the content contextual.

"Rushing around after the kids all day is tiring. Changing nappies, cleaning up their mess, cooking, and cleaning leaves you with no time. You'd love to have time to focus on your nutrition, but most of the time, you only have time for a quick smash-and-grab. You understand the principle of weight loss: consume fewer calories than you burn. But turning theory into practice is tough. So, here are 4 ways I help busy Mums like you maintain a calorie deficit and lose weight sustainably."

It's longer than I recommend most short-form videos, but you get the drift. In a couple of sentences, I've shown empathy. I've demonstrated that this piece of content is for a specific demographic. My target audience is likelier to stop and listen when the video appears in their feed. The same principle applies to the same topic but a different niche.

"Working 12-hour days and trying to hit project deadlines means nutrition is last on your agenda. You'd love to have time to meal prep and track every calorie. But most of the time, you only have time for a quick smash-and-grab at the Pret on the corner. You understand how to lose weight: consume fewer calories than you burn. Simple. But turning

theory into practice is tough. So, here are 4 ways I help busy working Mums like you maintain a calorie deficit and lose weight."

It's the same content, but I've made it relevant to a different target audience by using specific details.

Rule #2: Use relevant references, words, language, and images

It's vital to understand your niche beyond surface-level characteristics. Using the right words and phrases gives your content the *"they made this for me"* feeling.

To keep things consistent, I'll continue with the weight loss example. Imagine you're creating content for women who want to lose weight. These women don't want to get stuck in dieting hell. They want to enjoy themselves and still go out on the weekends. In this scenario, you wouldn't talk about guzzling ten pints of lager with the lads after the football. Instead, you might speak of sipping prosecco and dancing the night away. Yes. Yes. Yes. I've made a sweeping generalisation. But you have to play the percentages. Give me a break. I'm making a point.

The same principles apply to age-based references. If your audience is over 40, does your audience understand modern slang? I'm 42, and I had to Google "Bussin' Bussin'," "No cap," and "FR FR." And if you mention a music artist who didn't exist before 2001, there's a strong chance I don't know them.

It might be me. I'm too old. But lousy word choice and lazy references will alienate your audience.

Rule #3: Repeat the "Last 9" Test

The Last 9 test is something I recommend an online business does every month. We covered this earlier, but it's worth repeating. It's a vital sense check to ensure you're not straying from your strategy.

It's often too easy to get caught in the trap of creating content for the sake of it. You post daily to tick a box rather than make the right content for generating consistent leads. Stray from your strategy often enough, and your content drives your ideal clients away. Every month, look at your last nine posts and ask these questions.

1. Is it clear what niche you're targeting based on the headlines of your content?

2. Are the topics all relevant to your specific niche?

3. Have you used language that resonates with your ideal client?

If the answer to these questions is NO, there's work to do.

Revisit your strategy and pull yourself back on track. You don't need to make drastic changes. Make your next post one that's 100% perfect for your audience. Keep this course correction process in your diary every month. It will help you avoid disappearing down a two-month rabbit hole of lousy content.

Avoid Off-Brand Trends Like The Plague

For those who don't know their heavy metal history, Pantera is in the God Tier of metal bands. Throughout the '90s, Pantera pioneered a new sound—power groove. It was a heavy metal style that no band came close to replicating. Pantera stands alone—still.

The band had a raw, visceral, no-nonsense approach to music. Vocalist Phil Anselmo once addressed a live audience by saying,

"We're not gonna fucking blow nothing up. We're not going to have fucking lasers. We're not going to have fucking dragons jumping out of the PA. We ain't never been like that in our fucking lives. It's always been us, the music, the amps, the drums, and the fucking audience. And that's what makes it real."[2]

I thought about Anselmo's rant when soul-sucking trends started taking over social media. Creators, desperate for reach, likes, and views, abandoned all integrity. Pointless dancing, pointing, and lip-syncing replaced meaningful content. It's a trend that still persists. And as long as people value likes and views above all else, it won't disappear.

Trend-chasers have forgotten their goal isn't to grow a massive following at all costs. It's to communicate a specific, honest message to those needing help. Trending audio, dance crazes, and vacuous content are the equivalent of the pyros, lasers, and dragons Anselmo was rallying against.

Trends will come and go, as will the businesses that jump on bandwagons at a moment's notice. Remember, your audience isn't stupid. It's obvious when you create content for clicks. If a trend doesn't fit your brand values and voice, only one option exists. Avoid. Avoid. Avoid.

---

2. Anselmo, Philip H. (1999). Pantera 3: Vulgar Videos From Hell.

The Four Core Content Models For Each Major Format

Four core content formats dominate social media (at the time of writing). These are video, multi-slide posts, written posts, and live streams. I've created memorable frameworks for each format to help you create winning content.

Short-Form Video: SPAM Your Audience

I don't want you to create inane content your audience will detest. The double-SPAM formula gives you a simple structure for short-form video.

Succinct: Make the shortest, most concise version of your message. This doesn't mean every video needs to be less than ten seconds. Whatever the length of the video, ensure it's not one second longer than necessary.

Props: Standing in front of the camera is boring. And many viewers will struggle to retain information without visual aids. Use props to articulate your point, grab attention, and maintain interest.

Action: Get viewers to do something after watching your video. This could be as simple as liking the post or hitting the follow button. But, as you'll see in Part Two of the book, you will push for a lead nurturing action most of the time.

Movement: Delivering your message with the charisma of driftwood will kill your content. Add movement. It could be as simple as using hand gestures, adding jump cuts, or switching camera angles. As a general rule, make something happen every two seconds.

Now for your next set of SPAM tips.

Script: Script the first sentence of your video and plan the key things you want to say.

The first words out of your mouth are crucial. You'll lose viewers for good if you fail to hook them within the first 3-5 seconds. It's so vital that I've given you ten hook templates for short-form videos.

You can script the entire video, though it isn't essential. Most creators I work with prefer to list five to six bullet points for a 20-30-second video. This ensures you avoid repetition and waffle while keeping the video concise.

I've provided 10 opening hook templates on the next page. Use them for inspiration.

Point: One video. One point. This isn't the content format to make several meandering statements. Save the detailed content for articles, podcasts, and YouTube videos. Define the one thing you want viewers to remember, and focus on this, nothing else.

Accelerate: Don't dawdle. Unless your preamble grips attention like a best-selling novel, ditch it. Get to the point ASAP.

Make a fast exit: Don't dawdle on the way out. Once you've made your point, the video is over. Your audience isn't hanging around to hear you repeat everything. Make your point and go.

10 opening hook templates for short-form videos.

1. *"How Warren Buffett made his billions."*

Template: How [well-known business or celebrity] [desired goal].

2. *"Should you be eating cake if you're dieting?"*

Template: Should you be [action] if you're [process].

3. *"Here's the best way to avoid bad advice."*

Template: Here's the best way to avoid [undesirable thing].

4. *"Stop sending cold DMs to get leads. You need to do this instead."*

Template: Stop [common action]. You need to do this instead.

5. *"3 lessons from writing 2,353 emails I wish I'd learned earlier."*

Template: [Number] lessons from [event] I wish I'd known earlier.

6. *"I learned this sales tactic from my local butcher."*

Template: I learned this tactic from [unexpected source].

7. *"What NASA scientists can teach you about sales."*

Template: What [unusual source] can teach you about [goal].

8. *"If you're under 40 and broke, instead of..."*

Template: If you're [avatar] and [undesirable thing], instead of...

9. *"This is the most powerful copy framework I know."*

Template: This is the most powerful [topic] tactic I know.

10. *"The biggest mistake online businesses make with marketing is..."*

Template: The biggest mistake [avatar] make with [topic] is...

Multi-Slide Posts, i.e. Carousels: The PASTA Framework

Problem, Agitate, Solution (PAS) is a popular copywriting formula. Attention, Interest, Desire, Action (AIDA) is another. There's nothing wrong with these formulas. But they don't fit the multi-slide format on social media. I've adapted PAS to suit the psychology and behaviour of social media users. And, because everyone loves carbs, I called it PASTA.

The number of slides you could include in one post differs between platforms. The PASTA structure works regardless of the length of the post. To explain the framework, I'll use a ten-slide example.

Problem: This is the cover slide. Focus the headline on the issue the post helps solve. You can have short or long headlines. You can have subheadings. It doesn't matter. The only definitive rule is that it must be good.

Amplify: Use the second slide to dig deeper into the pain point. Show empathy and that you understand the problem.

Solution: This is the flexible part of the post. Increase or decrease the number of slides to suit your message and platform limits. Offer a solution to the problem. Don't hold back; give value.

Testimonial or Tease: In the penultimate slide, you connect the post topic to the CTA. You could offer social proof in the form of testimonials and transformations. For example, *"These 5 tips helped Susan land her first client and added £5k to her MRR. Here's what she had to say..."* The alternative is to tease the offer on the final slide. *"Need more help with [desired goal]? Swipe left one more time."*

Action: This is it. This is where you pitch your product or service and include a clear and concise call to action. Make what the prospects must do next simple, clear, and obvious.

Written Posts: All The Principles Apply

Written posts don't differ that much from other content formats. Your opening sentence is as vital in a caption as in a video. Sticking to one point is wise, as is being clear, concise, and avoiding waffling. You could even apply the PASTA framework.

The aspect of written posts to which you'll need to pay more attention is the CTA. It's the section people screw up. And it's the section that costs you leads and sales.

I use three simple principles to write compelling CTAs. I've also created a Copywriting for Social Media guide for this book. In it, you'll find headline templates, a list of high-converting words and phrases, and more. Head to poststoprofitsbook.com to grab your free copy.

Compelling CTAs: Tip #1: Benefits, Pain, and the So What? Test

Whether you're writing an email, sales page, caption, or carousel, at some point, you'll mention the features of your products and services. But here's the thing... No one cares about the features of what you're selling. Your potential customer only cares what those features can do for them. More specifically, they only care if those features make achieving their goal faster and easier. Sure, they'll spend 30 minutes of a 45-minute consult grilling you on *"what they get"*, but the truth is, they don't care. They might not know they don't care, but that's another story.

Think of it this way. If you could guarantee a potential client they could make £100k twice as fast as your competitors, they couldn't give a hoot whether you use a fancy app or the back of a McDonald's napkin to write their plan. Customers want results, and they want them as fast and as easy as possible.

So, you have to show them the benefit of the fantastic features. You have to join the dots and demonstrate how your weekly video consults will keep them more accountable than ever, ensuring they never go off-track or give up as they have in the past. Without benefits, features will never compel people to buy.

Talk about the benefits of your service in relation to how they help solve specific pain points. Tell people how the elements of your service make achieving their desired goal easier and faster. Do this, and not only will you have compelling CTAs, but you'll also have clarity about how best to sell your offer.

Make sure the benefits you write pass the "So What?" test. If you don't, your customers won't connect your words with a solution to their problem. And if this doubt exists, you won't make sales.

So What Test Step 1: List all the features of your product or service—for example, an app, weekly check-ins, a Facebook group, etc.

Example: You'll get access to my custom app.

So What Test Step 2: Note whether the feature helps prospects achieve their goal faster or easier. For example, an app containing a client's training programme makes building muscle easier.

Example: You'll get access to my custom app, which makes building muscle easier than ever.

So What Test Step 3: Match the feature to a pain point. Think about the pain points your customer struggles to overcome. Which of these challenges does each feature address? Write 1-2 sentences to show how their pain point disappears with your epic feature.

Example: You'll get access to my custom app, which makes building muscle easier than ever. Just open the app, and your entire training programme is waiting for you. All sets, reps, and weights are pre-programmed. I'll personalise everything based on your skill level and goal. It makes it easy to keep progressing in every session. All you need to do is turn up at the gym and follow the step-by-step instructions. There are even instructional videos for each exercise.

It takes all the thinking, frustration, and second-guessing out of the process. It's like having a personal trainer in your pocket (at a fraction of the cost).

To recap this example, the feature is an app. The basic benefit of the app is that it's convenient and makes training in the gym easier. The pain point it helps solve is someone's lack of understanding about what to do in the gym.

You will need to consider the character limit of captions when using this technique. But write the extended version and edit it as required for each platform.

Compelling CTA Tip #2: Make your CTA clear, simple, and obvious.

Use keywords so the prospect's next step is simple. "*DM me COACHING for more info.*"

You can also use the If/Then principle to generate desire and interest in your CTA. "*If you want to lose weight and keep it off for good, then DM me COACHING for more info.*"

Compelling CTA Tip #3: Use Persuasive Copy

Make it easy for people to say yes by overcoming objections using ethical persuasion. Here are six persuasive copywriting techniques.

Anchoring

Refer to a higher price point before introducing the price of your service. This juxtaposition makes your offer more value for money. Investing £100 a month might sound expensive. But, when you compare it to a service that costs £1,000 a month, it becomes a bargain.

"Going to the same level of detail with an in-person nutritionist will set you back at least £1,000/month. Online coaching comes in at just £100/month—a fraction of the cost."

"Up to"

Use the phrase "up to" when referring to potential results. It helps you avoid overpromising and giving impossible guarantees.

"Our typical clients earn up to £3,000 in their first 12 weeks."

"We've helped 764 businesses increase web traffic by up to 235% in just 6 months."

"Helps to"

Solutions aren't the function of one thing; they contribute. Use 'help to' so you don't mislead your audience.

"Walking at least 8k steps helps maintain a calorie deficit."

Bad Alternative

Make your service sound more appealing by comparing it to the competition. This is similar to anchoring. You're reminding the prospect of other available options. By anchoring the potential customer's thoughts to a negative alternative, your service becomes a more desirable choice.

"Awesome Life Coaching reverses the transformation process. Most coaches shoe-horn you into a fixed process, ignoring your well-being and circumstances. We work on sustainment first to create change from a solid foundation."

If/Then

Ask your audience if they want a specific outcome, and then tell them how to get it.

"Grab my new eBook if you want to lose up to 10kg in the next 90 days without giving up wine and pizza or piling it all back on."

Causality

Showing a logical path adds credibility.

"I know it's hard to find time to create when you're a company of one, and everything is your responsibility. That's why I created the 20-minute rapid content system. It'll help even the most time-crunched solopreneurs pump out lead-generating content in minutes."

Use these persuasion tactics with care. Integrity is everything. Don't lie to snatch a few leads now. Failing to deliver on your promises will kill your business before you realise it.

Going Live and Creating LSD Content

LSD Content bears no relation to Lysergic Acid Diethylamide. You're not going to start tripping before recording videos. That's the next book (that's a joke, in case any lawyers are reading).

LSD stands for Live. Splice. Distribute. I could've used a more straightforward name, but I like the idea of LSD Content catching on.

"Hey, Simon. Thanks for the advice, mate. I'm cranking up LSD production immediately."

It's the small things that make me happy. Here's a short summary of how LSD content works.

Live: Host a live stream on the platform where you get the most engagement.

Splice: Edit the live stream into short-form content.

1. Deliver the live on your smartphone.
2. Before starting the live stream, set up a different camera to film you doing the live stream.
3. Use an external microphone connected to your computer to record high-quality audio.
4. Edit the recording into short clips. You will need video editing software for this process.

You could download the live stream if it's an option, but the video and audio quality won't be great.

Distribute: Publish the micro-content across your social media channels.

This content creation method is nothing new. Gary Vaynerchuk, Joe Rogan, and others have published content this way for years. Although Joe and Gary have an army of social media creators. Your version is a little more rough and ready.

The benefit of LSD content is simple. A massive increase in content output with a significant reduction in the time taken to create it. Content nirvana.

At this point, I planned to guide you through the equipment and software you need to create LSD Content. But I'll be honest. I found it dryer than licking the sand dunes of the Sahara Desert. Don't get me wrong; it's excellent information. But explaining camera positions and cable choices is literary Xanax. So, I've created a simple free guide. Grab it at poststoprofitsbook.com.

The LSD approach isn't always easy to get right from the beginning. There's a high probability you'll make mistakes that make your micro-content useless. Here are eight tips to help you cook up the best LSD to get your audience high on your content supply.

Pick a topic: More people will watch your live if it's about a specific subject. Random Q&As work for those with a highly-engaged audience but not for most. Pick a problem your audience struggles to overcome and base your live on its solution.

Schedule the live: Based on my testing, I get almost double the number of people watching a live stream if I schedule it. So, ensure you promote the event in advance.

Plan the live: This is where you start to think about your LSD Content. I type 5-6 bullet points of things I want to cover during the live stream and keep these notes on my laptop. Plan to talk about the chosen topic for 10-15 minutes (longer if you want).

Think summary: Sometimes, you get carried away during live streams. No problem. But you need to make the editing process simple. After discussing each bullet point, pause for a 30-60-second summary. If the rest of the content is unusable, you haven't wasted your time.

Breathe: It's easy to rush through your content on a live stream. You don't get audible feedback, so it feels like a monologue. Pauses and silences often feel awkward, so you may feel pressured to keep talking. But this makes editing almost impossible. It's how you end up with 90-second clips that meander, always daring to make a point but never settling on one. Take your time, and breathe.

Plan the hook: Your micro content still needs an opening hook. Plan the hooks for each bullet point. This might seem strange and difficult to do on a live stream without looking forced, but it's possible.

Think Micro. Then Elaborate: Think about your micro-content first. Talk for 20-60 seconds as if you're summarising your message. Then, take the time to elaborate on your point for context and detail. You should get at least one solid piece of content this way. You may also get several more clips by elaborating.

Different camera angles and clothing: I don't know about you, but I have a lot of T-shirts that all look the same. Who likes having to make clothing decisions every morning? Not me. But when every clip looks the same, they're less watchable. I recommend switching things around between live streams.

With content creation done, it's time to post something. Don't worry. Don't be nervous. It's not a painful, tortuous process.

Chapter 14

STAGE 3: POST

The Six-Stage Content Strategy

> "Authentic brands don't emerge from marketing cubicles or advertising agencies."
>
> Howard Schultz

Imagine setting a goal of squatting 200kg. Logic tells you that achieving this goal takes time. The ideal plan doesn't involve loading 200kg on your back on day one and praying your knees don't break. You need to progress through phases of improving technique and increasing weight. Yet, many people don't apply the same logic to content creation. They want the end result from day one. They're unwilling to learn the skills needed to create high-quality content (at scale). And it doesn't take a genius to realise this is a lousy strategy. So, is the goal quantity or quality?

The simple answer is neither. Think of content creation as three evolutionary stages.

Stage 1: Volume. Post, and post often.

Fussing over the finer details of captions, thumbnails, fonts, and colours is pointless. When you start out, no one knows you exist. So, your first goal is to communicate your message as much as possible and get eyes on your content. This comes with volume.

Don't worry about having the best camera and the perfect lighting. It's not your priority. Neither is buying the same microphone Beyonce used on her latest album. Think down-and-dirty garage band, not multi-millionaire pop star. All you need is a smartphone, a good idea, and 20 seconds. Point it at your face and start talking. But don't publish complete rubbish. You must offer insights and opinions that resonate with your ideal clients.

Stage 2: Consistent volume with quality as a byproduct.

You might have read about the story of Professor Jerry Uelsmann. It's used in many business books to illustrate the importance of quantity over quality. Uelsmann divided his photography students into two groups: quantity and quality. He graded students in the "quantity" group based on sheer volume. Those in the "quality" group needed to produce one photo. But it had to be a near-perfect image to get the top grade.

At the end of the term, the results astounded Uelsmann. All the best photos came from the quantity group. The quality group spent their time discussing elaborate theories about the perfect image. But the "quantity" students experimented. They tested different compositions, lighting, and photographic techniques. Quantity produced quality.

At stage two, the goal is still quantity. Don't get distracted by pretty graphics and camera trickery. Think volume. Volume. Volume. Aim to post daily on your primary platform. Consistency allows your content to improve without much conscious effort. It's like "quality osmosis."

Distribute content across several platforms if you have the capacity. But don't waste time on the platforms your ideal clients won't use.

Stage 3: Producing high-quality content at scale.

Daily posting should be second nature if you've followed the process correctly. With daily content the norm, it's time for the final evolution—quality content at scale.

You've got plenty of data to analyse what works, what doesn't, and where to focus your efforts. So, now you can work on refining the quality of your content.

There are three core content skills you should look to improve:

Copywriting:

If you can write persuasive copy, you can create compelling content. But it's a complex skill to master, so prepare for a long road ahead. Here are three tips to start improving your copy chops.

Join the mailing lists of the best copywriters. Read everything they write. Think about what makes their writing so gripping. What is it about how they segue to an offer that compels you to click the link? How did they construct the subject line to make you open the email? Transfer what you glean to your captions, video scripts, and emails.

Read classic copywriting books. There's one book I'd recommend every budding copywriter read. *Breakthrough Advertising* by Eugene Schwartz. Buy it. Read it. Read it again. I've added a complete list of the best marketing books I've read to the resources available with this book. Head to poststoprofitsbook.com to grab your free copy.

Practise writing (with a bit of help). You can learn all the theory, but it counts for nothing if you don't put it into practice. Commit to writing often. And use writing software, like the Hemingway Editor, to help improve your copy.

Design:

If you're a novice designer, don't panic. Online software, like Canva, will make your life much easier. There's still a learning curve. But compared to the software the pros use, it's a breeze. And it's more than good enough for social media.

The more confident you become with the design, the more attention you can pay to the look of your posts. But don't spend hours designing a post when the twenty-minute version will perform just as well.

Video:

Video content's popularity continues to snowball. You'll need to learn a few basic skills to stay ahead of the trend. Don't worry. You're not recreating Schindler's List, so it won't take long to master jump cuts, captions, and zooms. You'll find plenty of online tutorials to help you navigate the basics.

Volume is your primary concern if you're at square one with content marketing. No doubt, you're fear of posting terrible content will lead you to procrastinate. But give yourself a slap and remember that these thoughts take you further from your goal.

Chapter 15

STAGE 4: INTERACT

The Six-Stage Content Strategy

"The best marketing strategy ever: CARE."

Gary Vaynerchuk

I'm on the I-80, heading west between NYC and Akron, Ohio. The booze is wearing off, and reality is setting in. This was supposed to be my time. This was everything I had been working for. Now, I'm crammed on a Greyhound bus with another sixty-eight hours to kill before we hit L.A. An old woman beside me is crunching Pringles as if she hasn't eaten in three weeks. I'm nursing a hangover, and all I hear is CRUNCH! Lip-smack. CRUNCH! Lip-smack. CRUNCH! Now I know what drives sane people to murder. If killing was my business, then business would be good right now. But it's not her fault. I'm angry, and everything is pissing me off. How did I not see this coming? I'm drinking with James, Lars, and Cliff one minute—shooting the shit over a few beers. The next minute, I'm on this fucking bus.

These are the made-up thoughts of Dave Mustaine. One of the founding members of heavy metal titans Metallica. In the early 80s, Mustaine and the rest of the band were in New York preparing to record their debut album, Kill' Em All. But in a cruel twist of fate, Mustaine's bandmates booted him out. Fuelled with anger and resentment, Mustaine formed a rival metal band, Megadeth. To date, Megadeth has sold more than 40 million albums worldwide. I triumph by any stretch of the imagination. But despite the band's evident success, Mustaine was never happy. The band that left him behind became the biggest metal act of all time. Metallica has sold over 125 million albums and plays to sell-out stadiums worldwide. The bay-area thrashers were the dark cloud overshadowing Mustaine's every move. In Mustaine's mind, every ounce of success was insignificant to what might have been. Rather than enjoy his achievements, Mustaine revelled in what he lost for decades.

It's the same comparison mentality that leads entrepreneurs to devalue their followers. There's a constant strive for more, more, more. But whether you have 1,000 or 100,000 followers, real people and potential clients are engaging with you. Don't dismiss these individuals because you're chasing more disciples to boost your ego. The more you treat your following as people, the more likely they'll become customers.

Don't believe me? Picture the scene...

You're standing in front of 1,000 people in an auditorium. The crowd isn't there to hear you sing or play the ukulele. People have gathered to listen to you speak. They want to hear your thoughts on the topics that interest them the most. They want insights, tips, opinions, and, with a bit of luck, a laugh or two. You step on stage and deliver your best stuff. As you come off stage, you're unsure if people enjoyed what you had to say. Then, someone taps you on the shoulder and says, *"There are 50 people waiting for you. They want to tell you how much they loved everything you said.*" Would that make you happy? Would that give you a good feeling? I imagine it would. Fifty people saying thank you is a big deal. But somehow, when we receive this gratitude online, it's dismissed as "low engagement." Madness! Unless you're hounded by crypto bots, everyone who watches a video or taps the like button is a real person. So, interact with them and treat them like humans. Trust me. If you can't appreciate 50 people, several thousand more won't make a difference to the success of your business. Comparison and expectation are the thieves of success.

Interaction doesn't mean spending hours on social media, doom-scrolling through inane content. You don't have to comment on every crackpot's post in the hope someone takes an interest in your content. Interaction, for interaction's sake, is banal. It's not even genuine interaction because you don't care about whom you're interacting with. You're doing it to tick boxes, please a shitty mentor, and try to rack up the Benjamins.

Interact with intent

Make your interaction on social media intentional. Remember, you are a creator first and a consumer second. Scroll through dog videos and the latest memes on your own time. When it's time to work, don't thumb through your feed because you can't resist seeing what everyone else is doing. You're stealing time from your business. Think about all the successful business owners you admire. How many of them make looking at what everyone else is doing a priority? Almost none. Curate your feed and make your social media environment work for you. It's a concept I used as a fitness and nutrition coach.

People struggle with temptation, and marketers know it. It doesn't matter what they're selling; brands know how to pull the right triggers. Take the humble doughnut, for example. The perfect mix of fat and sugar gives our brains a rush of *"I want more"* dopamine. Willpower is a weak defence against six freshly glazed doughnuts in the kitchen. An obvious way to overcome the temptation is to remove it. There's much less chance of munching through the doughnuts if you have to walk to the shop and buy them. Managing your environment helps develop good habits. The same goes for social media.

Start by switching off all notifications (except mine). You don't need to know when someone likes your post or sends you a message. The comments, DMs, and likes will be waiting for you when you decide to open the app. The platforms want you to spend time on their app, so they're set up to interrupt your day. Don't let it happen. Take control of your social media time.

Next, curate your feed. Mute accounts and posts you don't want to see in your feed. I muted almost everyone I follow while writing this book, even those who are personal friends. It wasn't because I disliked them or their content. I didn't want their thoughts and ideas to influence the concepts I was sharing. As soon as I've written the last word, I'll unmute them and carry on as usual.

You can curate your feed based on your current goals and objectives. And you can always go to a person's profile that you've muted to look at what they've posted. The difference is that you do it on your terms, not the algorithm's.

Think about your social media feed as a physical environment. As I type these words, I'm sitting in an empty co-working space. It's writing heaven. No distractions. It wouldn't be a haven if people kept coming to my desk to share their thoughts and opinions about myriad topics. My productivity would nosedive. It would be almost impossible to get any work done. Control your online interactions as much as you would your offline ones.

How to interact like a human

Am I patronising you? If I am, it's not my intention. Telling you to be human and treat people with respect seems like obvious advice. But I see entrepreneurs do the opposite all the time. So, as patronising as it might seem, I'll spell out the basics.

Every platform is different. And people use those platforms for different purposes. For example, Instagram is a "broadcast" platform. There's some conversation, but most creators broadcast their message to the world. Twitter is the opposite. Twitter is a "conversation" platform. It's less about curated content, professional videos, and perfect images. Most tweets are the fleeting thoughts and opinions of its users. You can see these differences in the way people interact with each other on the platforms. Twitter users engage in back-and-forth conversations. The value is the chat. On Instagram, many conversations happen in direct messages, not in the comments. Whatever platform you use, pay attention to how users expect to engage with you and your content. Make posts native to the platform, and match them to the expected user experience. You can't create one post and blast it to every platform. It might work for accounts with notoriety. Heck! Well-known creators could post an image of their morning ablutions and get engagement. You and I are not so lucky.

There are four primary ways to engage on any social media platform. There are more, but covering the basics will suffice for now. The first is simple: Say hello.

Say hello

What would you do if someone walked up to you in the street, tapped you on the shoulder, and said, *"Excuse me. I love that post you made yesterday..."* At first, it would be weird. You don't expect strangers to comment on your content while you're browsing shop windows. But, if it did happen, you'd say thanks. And, unless you had to be somewhere, you'd spend a few minutes chatting. So why wouldn't you do the same thing online? If someone taps the follow button or likes almost every post you make, a heartfelt thank-you goes a long way. Granted, as your account grows, it becomes a less manageable task. But it's a valuable use of your time in the early days. After all, you must use every advantage over the competition to stand out. Others with massive followings can't interact with everyone. But you can. So, give your audience more of your time.

I've decided not to give you templates for these messages. A robotic script detracts from the point of focusing on human interaction. Be yourself. Be interested in the other person, and be human. Still struggling? Here are five dos and don'ts.

1. **Use the person's name.** Take the time to click on their profile and personalise your message. A little effort goes a long way.
2. **Look at their profile.** Is there something on their profile or within their content you could reference? The same canned

response sent to 100 people lacks the personal touch.

3. **Never write *"Hey."*** You can spot a spammer a mile away when they send a one-word message that reads, *"Hey."* It's lazy. It's rude. And it assumes the recipient has the time or inclination to want to know what you have to say. Don't do it. The same goes for generic opening messages like, *"Is this the best place to ask a question?"* or *"I love your page. How long have you been..."* Stop! Stop! Stop! At least sleazy salesmen and women use marketing tactics that work. This? Well, I don't even know what this is. Avoid. Avoid. Avoid.

4. **Offer free help.** The fourth and fifth tips look like they contradict each other. But there are subtle nuances that make them both valid. Offering support in the DMs is a great way to start conversations. It's vital to approach these messages without expectation. You aren't trying to guide someone to a sale. Remember, you are being human and showing interest. This doesn't mean you can never mention your service, but wait for the right time. Send a message like this, *"Hey, [insert name]. Thanks for the follow. I really appreciate it. I'm guessing you noticed I'm a marketing coach. Are you struggling with any aspect of your social media marketing? I'm happy to offer a few free tips if I can help."* You *could* use this as a template. But I tried to make it generic and force you to think for yourself. When the person replies, direct the person to a helpful post, article, video, or download. Provide the free help you promised. You can follow up later if a conversation about your service would help them.

5. **Never coach in the DMs.** There's a fine line between giving

value and coaching people for free. The latter is a lead-killer, so knowing the difference is essential. Giving value is sharing concepts, ideas, opinions, and insights. Coaching is the nuanced implementation of those concepts to someone's specific circumstances. For example, this book is chock full of value (ok, it wasn't free, but the same rule applies). It's a low-cost way to access all my thoughts and ideas on social media. But, if you slide into my DMs asking for detailed advice to implement these ideas, the answer will be (a polite) no. It devalues my service and courses and is disrespectful to my paying clients. Set the boundary, and most people will respect it. Have no limits, and people will traipse their shit into your DMs.

Comment to converse

Lazy commenting is one of the fastest ways to tell your followers you don't care. When people take the time to post a meaningful thought, the least you can do is reply. After all, it's in your interest. Not only will it help build connections with your audience, but it has a positive effect on the algorithm. More interaction leads to more reach, which leads to more interaction. It's a positive cycle that you can kick start by taking a minute to reply to comments.

The secret to good comments is conversation. Reply to a comment with a question or thought-provoking statement. Striking up a genuine conversation with your audience starts a snowball effect. But be genuine. People will sniff out an insincere attempt to hack the algorithm at their expense. So, blend this marketing tactic with a genuine interest in the individual and what they have to say.

Use platform features to your advantage

Social media platforms contain features that make relationship-building simple. Certain content formats often constrain your thinking. You have to say everything within a few thousand characters or under thirty seconds. Anything longer, and you risk losing attention. But a live stream is different. Hosting a live Q&A session is perfect for giving more detail and context to your ideas. Your audience expects you to talk for ten, fifteen, twenty minutes, or more. This allows followers to get to know you, your character, and how you deliver your service.

Good content marketing breaks down the barrier between your prospects and your service. Those barriers crumble when you show them what it's like to work with you. After that, the sale is much easier.

Many platforms also offer interactive Q&A options. No doubt you've used them. And if you've got a small or unresponsive following, you've undoubtedly dealt with the shame of no replies. But don't lose hope. The solution is often the question you ask.

As most couples do, I often chat with my wife about what to have for dinner.

"What do you fancy for dinner, Maria?" It's a simple, innocuous question.

"Oh, I don't know. Anything. I'm not fussy." I've come to learn that this is a lie. Maria does know, and she is fussy. I'm asking the wrong question. But in my naivety, I reply...

"How about steak?"

"No. It's too heavy. I'm not that hungry." She replies. Hinting at what she wants like it's a cryptic crossword.

"How about chicken salad?" This is my next effort. It's lighter, but filling. The perfect solution. Or is it?

"No. It's a bit boring."

And so the endless loop goes until we settle on whatever Maria knew she wanted in the first place.

You get digital tumbleweeds when you ask loose, ill-defined, non-specific questions. *"Ask me a question"* only works if you have a responsive audience that loves asking you stuff. You can cultivate this relationship, but it won't happen overnight. In the meantime, ask more "negative" questions.

"What is your biggest struggle with writing copy?"

"What one thing frustrates you most about building a business?"

"What's the one problem you've struggled to solve for months?"

Phrasing questions in this way leads people into a narrow thought process. It's a technique that boosts question replies and stops you from feeling like you're talking to yourself.

Hack the network

The fastest way to grow your social media audience is to ethically steal someone else's. Paid advertising is faster, but that's for another book.

My audience comprises coaches, creators, and entrepreneurs with service-based businesses. I'm the guy who takes you from an idea to consistent leads. I'm honest and say that I don't teach people how to conduct sales calls. There are others better placed to teach you the art of sales. So, there is an obvious opportunity for a sales expert to offer value to my audience (and vice versa). Through a social media Q&A, podcast, or webinar, I would give the right sales expert access to my audience.

Speaking to thousands of your ideal clients would take months through organic content. Networking is the accelerant that fast-tracks the process. Choose collaborations wisely, and you'll build an avid audience of potential buyers. (P.S. This isn't an open invitation for salespeople to slide into my DMs. It's an example).

Start networking by making a list of three types of people.

1. **Your Peers.** Accounts and businesses who have a similar sized following.

2. **Those ahead of you.** These people do what you do but have been doing it longer.

3. **The shot-in-the-dark.** These are the unicorns of your industry. The people who everyone admires. Don't expect to jump on their social media any time soon. But, as you progress up the networking ladder, you're more and more likely to bag a unicorn or two.

I'm going to let you in on a secret. It's a way to edge up the network pyramid faster. Ask each collaborator you work with to connect you with someone in their network. You're looking for audiences who would find your content valuable. So be selective. If you get a positive response, ask them to introduce you via email or DM. The introduction reduces the likelihood of getting ignored.

You'll notice that cold outreach isn't on my list of tactics. This isn't to say it doesn't work. But spamming 50 people a day with a generic canned message isn't my idea of fun. And whilst cold DMs might "work," if it comes at the expense of your integrity and longevity, was it even worth it? Never forget that people are savvier and can spot a sales pitch a mile away. So, lead the spam-free revolution and be more honest in your marketing. It's a crazy idea, but it might catch on.

Chapter 16

STAGE 5: GENERATE

The Six-Stage Content Strategy

"Lead magnets are the bridge between "Hi" and "Buy."

Simon Mitchell

It was the best of lead magnets. It was the worst of lead magnets. Since starting my first online business, I've used every lead magnet imaginable. I've written eBooks, created video courses, delivered webinars, and offered free trials. And I've lost count of how many 5-day challenges I've facilitated. Most of my lead magnets were great resources packed with information. But, despite the value, most of them failed to generate consistent leads. Many entrepreneurs suffer from the same problem. Creating a high-value resource you can't even give away is frustrating.

Through trial and error, I realised there are three elements to a successful lead magnet. Use these for lead-generating power stronger than the Death Star's tractor beam.

- The Domino Principle

- Time to Value
- Nurture Accelerator

The so-called experts and I agree on one thing. Posting on social media is essential for almost every online business. The downside is that it's unpredictable. Even if you mix great content with a huge dollop of luck, you might reach 20% of your followers on a good day. Putting all your faith in uncontrollable algorithms is insanity. Instead, combine your organic content with email marketing.

It makes sense. Social media is for value-driven, customer-focused lead generation. Email is for nurturing, building trust, and making sales. But something is missing. You need a bridge between social media and your email list. Enter... The Lead Magnet.

A lead magnet is a resource you give away in exchange for an email address.

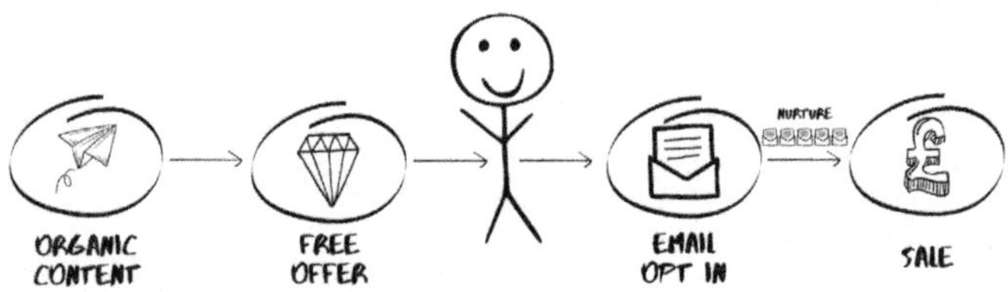

Your lead magnet is the bridge between problems and solutions. It's the stepping stone that turns followers into warm leads.

"Why grab an email address? Isn't email dead?"

Oh no, no, no, my young Padawan! Email marketing isn't dead. It's fighting fit and ready to open a can of whoop-ass on delusional social media "experts." More on that later. For now, let's concentrate on choosing the right lead magnet.

There are many types of lead magnets, and knowing which to use is confusing. Some marketers love webinars and their ability to convert prospects with relative ease. Others extoll the benefits of eBooks, cheat sheets, and free trials. After all, they're often quick and easy to create, meaning you can start generating leads fast. But, the format of the lead magnet is not your first consideration.

The effectiveness of your lead magnet—whether it generates leads—lies in its topic. Choose the wrong subject for your lead magnet, and it won't matter which format you use. No one will want it.

Finding the right lead magnet starts with your Problem Path. You know... the thing you mapped out in Part One of the book. You did map it out, right?

The Domino Analogy

Your lead magnet must meet your ideal customer where they are at. I wouldn't offer you an email automation guide if you struggled to define your avatar. The guide would contain valuable information, but it doesn't help you now, which makes it a lousy lead magnet.

Imagine the problems your ideal client faces are a line of dominoes. The last domino represents success—the final goal. The first domino represents their most significant, immediate problem. Your aim is to develop a lead magnet that helps knock over the first domino.

It often helps to think about what happens when you start working with a new client. What problem jumps to the top of the priority list most often? Aim to make your lead magnet a full or partial solution to this immediate problem.

Helping prospects to make a breakthrough builds trust, authority, and reciprocity. These are essential persuasion triggers that will increase your chances of making sales.

Time To Value

Your lead magnet must give value. Your prospects will feel cheated into receiving your marketing communications if it doesn't. The goal is to deliver a lightbulb moment as fast as possible.

Time to Value (TTV) is the lag between opting in for a lead magnet and getting benefits from that lead magnet. For example, it won't take long to get value from a well-written five-page eBook with lots of great tips. The TTV is short. But, if I have to wade through a *"93-page Ultimate Guide"*, there's a high chance I won't make it to the end and get all the benefits. Even though the value is high, the TTV is long. And the longer the TTV, the higher the probability prospects will lose interest and move on.

Time to Value is one element of a bigger equation.

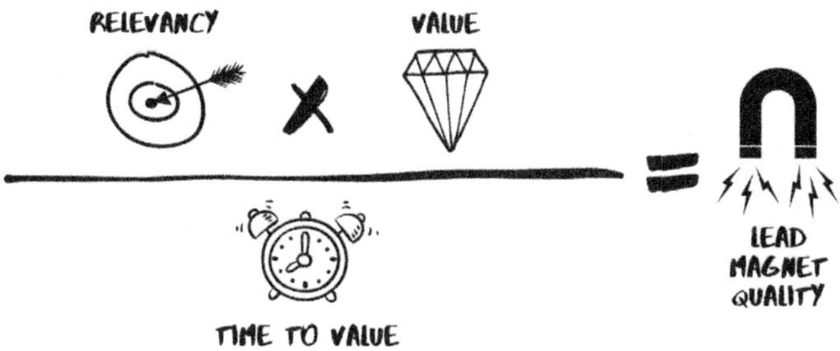

The other other factors in the equation are the degree of value and the lead magnet's relevancy. The more value you give in the shortest time, the greater your chances of increasing lead quality. It's a simple equation. Relevancy multiplied by Value, divided by Time to Value.

Relevancy denotes how relevant the lead magnet is to the prospect's immediate problem. Value is the degree to which the lead magnet helps solve the immediate problem. Note that value also takes into consideration your proficiency with the chosen format. Value will decrease if you write an eBook but lack writing skills. And the value will increase if you have the on-camera skills of Robert De Niro and decide to record a webinar. The final part of the equation is Time to Value. TTV is the time taken to realise the perceived value.

Imagine you were deciding between a 30-minute webinar and a 50-page eBook. For argument's sake, both lead magnets have the same relevancy and value—10 and 8 out of 10, respectively. But there is a vast discrepancy in TTV. The webinar's TTV is thirty minutes, so you give it a TTV value of two. The eBook takes about three times as long to read. So, its TTV is much higher—six. (These numbers are arbitrary, by the way). Then, plug these numbers into the formula to assess which has the greater chance of success.

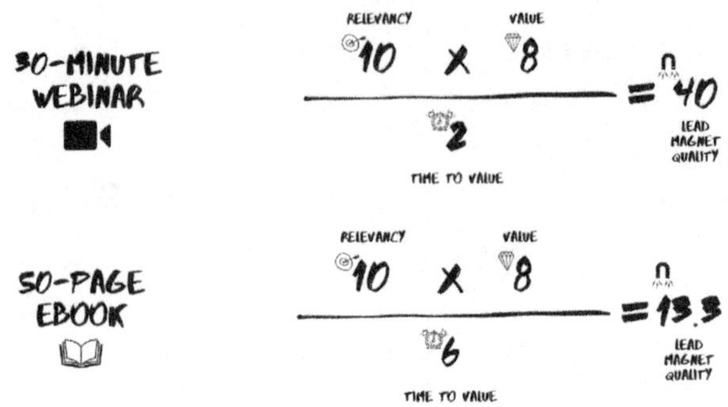

The formula hasn't endured years of scientific testing. It's a crude method to assess what lead magnet to produce. It's one tool I use to make faster and more accurate decisions. And for the record, I'm not saying that eBooks are bad and don't generate quality leads. The point is the faster you deliver a relevant, high-value result, the further down the buying journey they start.

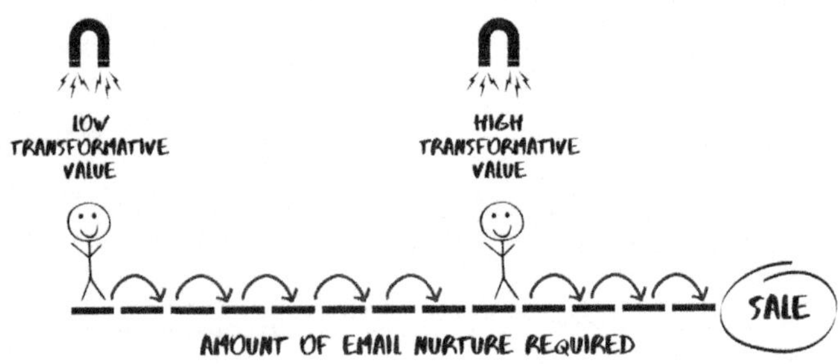

Lead magnet examples

You can use dozens of lead magnets to attract your ideal clients. Here are eleven of the most common:

- eBook

- Cheat sheet
- Physical book
- Free 5-day or 7-day challenge
- Free trial
- Scorecard
- Quiz
- Client case study
- Live webinar
- Pre-recorded webinar
- Sample of a course

It's impossible to tell you which lead magnet to use. The answer depends on you, your niche, and the problem(s) your service solves. Use the formula to compare options.

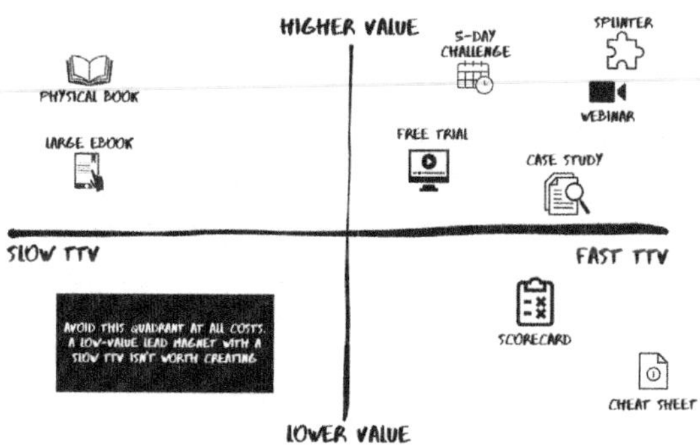

To help you create better lead magnets, I've detailed three lead magnets below. First, I'll show you how to build a Client Case Study webinar. This style of lead magnet is perfect if you are selling high-ticket offers. Next, one for the online course creators. I used a Splinter Funnel to promote my course, Social Launch. It outperformed every lead magnet I've tried. I'll show you how it works from start to finish. Third, I'll show you how to use Scorecards for low-ticket offers and data-rich sales calls.

The Chet Holmes Buyer's Pyramid shows that only 10% of your audience is ready to buy.[1] The rest are either not thinking about it or know they don't want what you're selling. Targeting the 10% of potential buyers with your lead magnet is crucial. Trying to convert every follower into a lead is a fool's game.

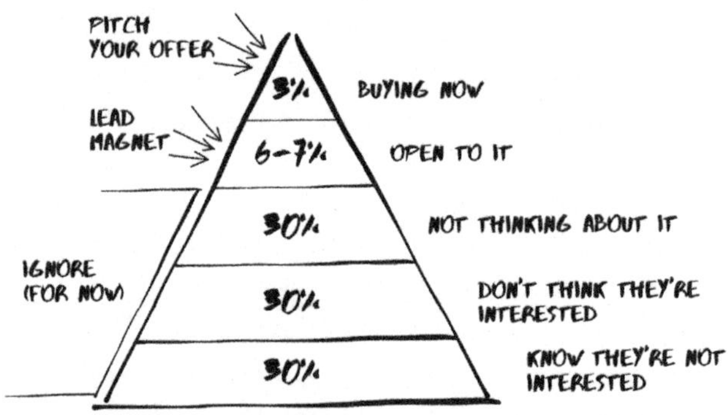

There are inherent flaws in using low-quality lead magnets to sell high-ticket offers. Low-quality lead magnets often attract low-quality leads. Be warned! You could be building an email list of tyre kickers.

---

1. Holmes, Chet. (2008). The Ultimate Sales Machine: Turbocharge Your Business with Relentless Focus on 12 Key Strategies

Client Case Study:

One of the best lead magnets to sell high-ticket offers is the Client Case Study. A webinar would work in the same situation by refocusing the topic of the presentation. One of my private 1:1 clients, Jewade, used a Case Study lead magnet to attract new leads and grow his online coaching business with relative ease. He started getting qualified leads every week, even though he had less than 900 followers. Within six months, he had a solid client base and consistent leads. He quit his job as an in-person trainer and went all-in on his online business. Still think you need a massive following for effective social media marketing?

When I started working with Jewade, we discussed several lead magnet options. Jewade is an experienced Personal Trainer who mentors other trainers. He had the skills and the process to achieve jaw-dropping results. Every. Single. Time. As I looked through his transformations, I scratched my head thinking... *"How does he get results like this so often?"* It's like he has a 'Get Shredded' conveyor belt. Put the client on one end. Out pops a jacked, shredded, knowledgeable trainer in 16 weeks. The lightbulb went DING! If I'm wondering how he does it, I bet his prospects are, too.

At the time, Jewade's client, Rich, had completed a transformation several weeks earlier. It was the perfect opportunity to create an end-to-end case study. The goal was to show his prospects his entire process. If people could see the process, they could imagine themselves going through it. In hindsight, it worked even better than we hoped.

First, it was simple and quick to create. No complicated webinar software or time spent writing a lengthy eBook. We created a simple presentation deck and recorded a video using free software. The hidden benefit was that they were already sold when prospects booked a call. Potential clients knew Jewade's process, what they got, how it worked, and even the estimated value of the coaching package.

Jewade is converting almost every sales call into a client. The call isn't much of a "sales" call, either. It's more a sense check that the client is a good fit. You could say Jewade is interviewing them, not the other way around. Plus, because prospects have seen the process in the lead magnet, there's no lull in the sales call. Jewade doesn't have to explain how every component of coaching works. The lead magnet did the grunt work. Here's a step-by-step breakdown of constructing a case study lead magnet.

The Cover

A great cover combines the image of the client's result with a strong headline. If you don't deliver physical transformations, get creative. You also need a solid headline to attract people on social media. Jewade chose, ***'How Busy PT & New Dad Rich Lost 10kg and Got Cover Model Ready In 15 Weeks."*** It's not perfect, but it does the job.

The Beginning

After a short agenda slide, creating a vivid picture of the client's starting point is crucial. You must detail their struggles and challenges. Focus on a critical point of frustration that most prospects will share. Also, show your process. Create a visual of all your clients' essential steps on their journey.

The Middle

This is your domain. Tell people exactly what you did to create the transformation. Don't be shy. Show them everything.

Ensure you relate every step of the transformation to the stages of Unique Mechanism. Aim to show the direct correlation between progress and the structure of your process. The more you can reinforce that your approach works, the more leads you'll convert.

The Switch to the Pitch

Start by showing more client results. Pile on social proof with more images that show your process works. Take the opportunity to remind people of your process. Repeat the visual from earlier in the presentation. Once you've done that, give people two options.

"Option 1: I could leave you with this basic framework that you can apply yourself. Without my guidance, I can't guarantee it'll work, but if you go down this route, I wish you the best of luck.

Or... Option 2: I can take an active role in helping you achieve the same jaw-dropping results. I can provide accountability, motivation, and support. I can take the frustration out of the process and give you the tools to sustain the results for years to come."

The Pitch

At the end of the presentation, you must pitch your no-brainer offer. Don't be timid. If you're going to sell, SELL! Sell with pride, passion, and belief.

Jewade lists everything clients get when they join and the benefits of each feature. You can add the financial value of each element if you intend to share the price during the presentation. But, if your CTA is a sales call, remove pricing unless you have massive authority. You might scare potential buyers away.

Add legitimate scarcity to your pitch if you can. Limited spaces, limited-time pricing—anything that will force people to decide.

Splinter Funnel

It sounds like a Tom Clancy novel or the 189th book in the Jack Reacher series. But, believe it or not, The Splinter Funnel is one of the most effective ways to attract the right clients.

In January 2023, I started using The Splinter Funnel as my only lead magnet. Within three months, this simple offer generated 528 qualified organic leads. Not only did it boost email subscribers, but it also paid my mortgage for the next 4 months. Not bad for a product that took no time to create.

Purists will say that The Splinter Funnel isn't a lead magnet because it's not a free offer. But I'm uninterested in these semantics. Yes, the prospect pays to access the lead magnet. But I don't care about this small revenue stream. It's what an investment, however small, does to the buying relationship. Don't get me wrong. There's a place for free lead magnets. The Splinter Funnel might not be what your business needs. You might not have a product that suits the strategy. But it's worth considering, especially if you're an online course creator.

A paid lead magnet makes sense for several reasons (four, to be precise). First, you make money, which is never a bad thing. Instead of giving everything away for free, you get a little money from every opt-in.

Second, you create a buying relationship from the outset. It's often difficult to switch from giving free value on social media to getting people to invest. It's almost as if they see you as the "freebie-giver." You're the friendly, generous person who gives stuff away for free. You're not the big, evil, money-grabbing ogre. Getting prospects to dip their hand in their pocket doesn't turn you into a money-grabber. But it does put potential clients in the mindset that investing in you brings reward.

Third, people buying the lead magnet are far more likely to use what you're selling. I have (as I'm sure you have to) downloaded freebies, only for them to gather digital dust on my hard drive. The content could be the most transformative, life-changing content, but I'll never know. I didn't have skin in the game. I didn't invest anything. There were no consequences to ignoring the freebie and moving on with life. Charging people for a lead magnet is in their interest and yours. You're doing your audience a favour by making them part with their cash.

Fourth, people who buy are also far more likely to buy more. Objections disappear if your ideal clients sample your service with almost no risk. You allay fears, doubts, and concerns. You prove you're not a scammer or charlatan. Potential customers get a result before making the investment that completes the job.

You're sold. I can feel it. A lead magnet that helps you make more sales while paying the mortgage sounds great. So, let me tell you how The Splinter Funnel works, starting with a one-sentence summary.

The Splinter Funnel is the "unboxing" of your offer and giving away one part for a crazy low price.

I'll use Social Launch to show you how The Splinter Funnel works.

Unbox your offer

To make a Splinter Funnel, you must first unpack your offer.

Your main product or service will comprise several components. You wrap everything into one package and sell it to your ideal customers. For example, courses often include several modules with dozens of lessons and resources. You could unbox and choose any of these elements for a Splinter Funnel.

Social Launch is my flagship online course. It helps online businesses get more leads from social media. The in-depth modules guide people through the Posts to Profits process. Each module has a 60-90-minute video training, workbooks, cheat sheets, templates, and more. Plus, I give away bonus courses and training worth over £3k to sweeten the deal. Each of the modules is a possible splinter. The question is, which one is the best choice?

Choose your splinter

The sexiest, coolest-sounding, attention-grabbing part of your offer should be the splinter. It's got to solve one of your ideal customer's immediate problems. It must help them overcome failure (to some degree) and get them off square one. My decision was straightforward.

I've structured Social Launch so that each module builds on the next. Skipping to Module 4 without completing the previous lessons leads to one thing... shitty results. Making the first module of the course my Splinter Offer was an easy decision.

Your Splinter Offer must also create a sense of *"Holy shit! I want that"* in the prospect's mind. It must be jaw-dropping. You want people to think you've lost your mind. Like you're a character Ken Kesey deleted from One Flew Over The Cuckoo's Nest for being too out there.

To create the *"Holy shit!"* offer, I included all the bonuses, templates, and workbooks... Everything. I thought about offering the bonuses as an upsell. But it detracted from the offer's wow factor. So, I left them in and looked at other ways to boost sales (more on that later).

Price your splinter

Pricing your splinter offer is simple. Keep it under £10. The single-digit price makes people take notice. Plus, almost everyone can afford £10 for something that can solve a huge problem. But offering a product at a low price doesn't always have people rushing to part with their cash. Prospects might think what you're offering is too cheap. After all, you get what you pay for. So, the trick is to show a credible price drop. Here's a step-by-step walkthrough.

I've never sold modules of Social Launch outside of the packaged course. I had to think about what I would charge if I did and ensure the price was believable. In the end, I settled on £299. Dropping this to £5 meant customers saved 99%. Next came the bonuses:

Algorithm Hacker Blueprint. This was a 90-minute training detailing the inside secrets of Instagram algorithms. Creators could leverage the knowledge to post content that generates more likes, leads, and sales. This course sold for £99 when I first released it.

Canva Templates Mega Bundle. I collated all my Canva templates and put them into one mega bundle. It helped entrepreneurs with no design skills create pro-level content overnight. Based on previous selling prices, the template packs in this bundle totalled £110.

10 x Flight Plan Digital Back Issues. I write a monthly newsletter called Flight Plan. The newsletter gives subscribers the latest social marketing strategies, insights, and tactics. It's a behind-the-scenes look at the inner workings of my business. A digital subscription to Flight Plan costs £49/month. So, ten issues total £490.

The combined Splinter Offer:

Social Launch: Module 1 = £299.

Algorithm Hacker Blueprint = £99.

Canva Template Mega Bundle = £110.

10 x Flight Plan Digital Back Issues = £490.

TOTAL = £998 Splinter Offer = £5 (99.5% off).

The offer is insanely valuable. But every price is logical and believable. Valuing each component at £997 would sound impressive. But it's likely to cause prospects to doubt mine, and the offer's, integrity.

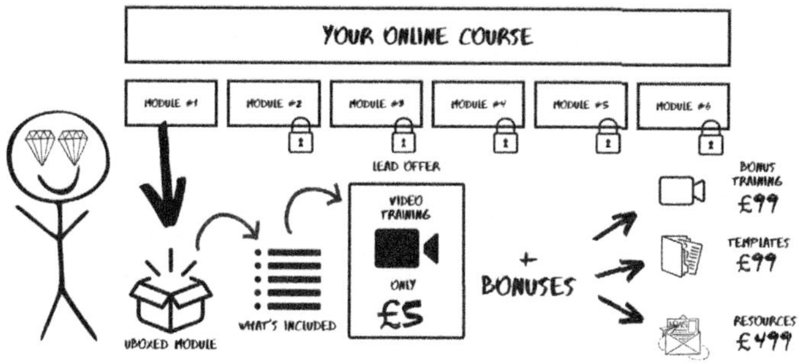

Name your splinter

I love names that focus on the result people achieve if they apply everything. So, I focused on one aspect of the training that teaches coaches how to get leads from story highlights. This technique helps get leads on autopilot... Hence, Leads On Autopilot. Everyone wants leads, and everyone wants them with minimal work. Perfect!

Use the naming approach I gave you in the offer section of the book to decide what you'll call your Splinter offer.

Order Bumps, Upsells, and the one-time offer

Selling £5 lead magnets is great, but it's not the main aim. The goal is to upsell customers to other products and services. This is where order bumps, upsells, and a one-time offer is crucial.

Order Bumps

Order bumps are offers that appear at the checkout before the customer purchases. They're like snacks you see at supermarket checkouts while queuing to pay. They're the low-cost, no-brainer items you throw into your basket at the last minute. This makes them seem unimportant, but that couldn't be further from the truth. The order bump in my Splinter Funnel generates 50% more revenue than the £5 offer. 15% of people buying the Splinter Offer add the order bump to their cart. The trick to a successful order bump comes down to three things:

- Relevancy.
- Price.
- Copy.

The order bump MUST be relevant to the primary offer. It needs to make achieving the desired result faster and easier. A random promotion might work, but sales will be sporadic and unreliable. My order bump was a mini-course, Social Media Sales Formula. It was a training I created specifically for the funnel. It guides people through the process of making sales from social media. I knew that making sales was a logical progression if people wanted leads.

Next up, price. I've tested order bump pricing on previous offers. Anything below £50 performs well with lower-priced offers. You can push this higher if your primary offer is more expensive. But, people are unlikely to buy a £997 course from a £5 offer. Use a little common sense. I valued the training at £299 and gave customers 85% off the price at the checkout.

The third essential component is the sales copy. You can't write a 5,000-word sales page on a checkout page, so you must be succinct. It's crucial to include scarcity. Make customers aware that this is the ONLY time they'll see the offer at this price. If they miss it, they miss out. And follow through on that statement. Don't allow people to email you a few days later and give them access to the offer. Ensure your scarcity is as real as it gets.

Upsells

Upsells are offers that appear after the initial checkout process. You provide several related offers to help increase how much each customer spends. The general rule is to include 2-10 upsells per funnel. Although, any more than four feels like overkill. It makes for a frustrating experience that leaves customers cursing your name. Here are the bones of my approach. FYI. This isn't the only way to structure upsells, but it's a way that works.

Lead with a one-time offer for your main product or service. This is where you "rebox" your offer and allow customers to buy the complete package at a limited price. In my Splinter Funnel, customers have one chance to buy the entire Social Launch course at 50% off. If they say no, they'll never see that price again.

They may receive 40% and 25% discount offers further into the funnel. But the 50% discount is a one-time offer. Miss it. Miss out. Don't expect massive sales unless you're a household name. People are buying the low-cost teaser to sample the goods. Leaping straight to purchasing your complete solution is unlikely for most people. But you can sweeten the deal with a solid money-back guarantee.

I give coaches 28 days to sample Social Launch. They'll get a full refund if they don't think it's worth the money. So, they can take advantage of the one-time offer and sample everything risk-free. I've made it the smart move to buy the upsell.

Descending price If you have more than one upsell, structure them in descending price order. The higher-priced offer creates an anchor from which everything else seems much cheaper. For example, 50% off Social Launch means customers pay £498. If they reject that offer, they'll see an offer for my Email Swipe File Hub, priced at £149. Then, they see my design course, Canva Content Mastery, for £97. And finally, a Flight Plan subscription for £79/month. Versus £498 for Social Launch, all the subsequent offers feel like a steal.

Descending importance

When creating the funnel, my main products were Social Launch, Social Launch 2, and Flight Plan. This might make you question why the Flight Plan subscription is at the end of the upsell sequence. Why not put it straight after the Social Launch offer? Well, it's for two reasons.

One. People don't like subscriptions. Even though you can cancel anytime, it's a more significant commitment than a one-off payment. With this knowledge, I knew that Flight Plan upsells in this funnel would be low. So, I put them at the end of the funnel.

Follow-up

The first 30 days after buying are crucial. You want customers to consume the content and sample the service. This is the window where conversions are highest if you do things correctly. A follow-up email sequence is essential. More on this in the next section.

TL:DR?

In case you nodded off, here's the short version.

Take the sexiest, most attention-grabbing part of your offer and give it away for a crazy-low price. Don't hold back. Give the training videos, the workbooks, and the cheat sheets. Everything except your time. When prospects consume a valuable chunk of your offer, it's like taking a bite of the gooiest, most delicious brownie... but then having it whipped away as your spoon descends for another bite. To be blunt. You're teasing your audience.

But... and it's a big but (I cannot lie), the taste must be sweeter than gloops of warm caramel over those fresh brownies. They won't return for more if it leaves a sour taste in your prospect's mouth.

Scorecards:

Before we get into the detail, let me rewind the clock. It's March 2023. My Splinter lead magnet is generating leads every week. But I've promoted it daily for 12 weeks straight. Almost every post between January and March had a CTA to buy the first module of Social Launch for £5. It was a crazy offer—the definition of a no-brainer. After focusing on this lead magnet for 3 months, most of my (engaged) organic audience bought the offer. So, it was time to start thinking of a new way to attract fresh leads.

I experimented with Scorecard Marketing in the past with limited success. But, at the time, I had too much going on to devote the time to making it work. There was no strategy, no plan, and as a result... no leads. Fast forward to 2023, and things were different. I understood more about how you can use this tool to nurture leads.

The Pain

Your quiz must, must, must focus on a pain point. No one will take your quiz for shits and giggles. Well, they might, but I wouldn't pin your hopes on consistent leads.

Your quiz should focus on the immediate pain your ideal client faces. Put yourself in their shoes and figure out why they are stuck. But pain alone doesn't make a compelling lead magnet.

The Promise

Your prospects won't want to answer questions that lead nowhere. No matter how small, you must offer a result. Take my Content Health Check (which you can access at poststoprofitsbook.com), for example. Prospects get a personalised report and the next steps to solve their marketing problems. It's a high-value output for 90 seconds of effort.

The Purpose

You want your quiz funnel to generate leads; that's obvious. But start thinking about the bigger picture.

You want to make the process of attracting and converting those leads easier. You want your lead generation machine to whirr in the background while you do other things. This is why you need a strategy—a defined outcome.

A quiz funnel allows you to find the nuances in your niche. It enables you to segment your audience into micro-niches. With granular data, you can deliver more targeted, relevant marketing to increase conversions.

Structure

Keep the quiz simple. The goal is to get people to complete it, not abandon it after you ask your 187th question. After testing several options, I've found that c.25 yes/no style questions work well. The yes/no style is easy for people to answer. They don't have to type anything or overthink their response. You can include a few rating-style questions to vary the style.

"Ok, Simon. But what questions do I ask?"

Well, that's the... err... million-dollar question!

The questions must allow you to categorise the prospect. You might segment people based on skill level, knowledge, or what point in the journey they are stuck.

My Content Health Check mirrors the Posts to Profits process. The process has five sections: Basics, Strategy, Leads and Sales, Consistency, and Mastery. I can make broad assumptions of strengths and weaknesses from someone's responses. This allows me to segment my leads and deliver targeted follow-ups. Think about the questions you have to ask to segment your audience.

The last part of your quiz to consider is the output—what you'll give people on completion. I provided a customised report with extra information and suggested next steps.

You could also send a short video series tailored to each outcome. As with most things, there is more than one correct answer. So think about the format your audience will love.

Segmentation

Now comes the critical part. You must tailor your email follow-up based on the quiz responses. If you don't, there was no point in creating the quiz. Think about the specific problems of your segmented audience. Then, create separate email sequences with appropriate offers. Need an example? Oh, ok then. Here are the tailored offers I used to offer.

Red = First module of Social Launch for £5.

Amber = One-time discount on the entire Social Launch course.

Green = 1:1 Mentorship promotion.

Data-rich Follow-Up

Whether you're booking sales calls or following up with prospects on social media, use the quiz responses. You can ask more focused, personalised questions, leading to more meaningful conversations. More data = More conversions.

"I saw you scored a 9 on strategy but a 2 on leads. Do you feel like your strategy isn't working?" It's a much more effective way to ask questions than, *"So, tell me, what's your biggest problem?"*

The TASK Method. How to promote your lead magnet on every post without being spammy.

Every social media post has two purposes: one for the prospect and one for you.

Your prospect is selfish. People want something in return for their attention. So, you must educate, entertain, and solve their problems. You don't need to dance, point, and sell your integrity for engagement. The latest dance craze might get thousands of views, but they're not meaningful views. People aren't buying high-ticket coaching because you have dope dance moves. Unless, of course, you're a dance teacher.

You also want something out of the post. Your goal is to progress the relationship with your prospects. You want to inch people closer to a sale. Doing so will help these people, so it's for their benefit that you have selfish interests. The trick is balancing these competing outcomes in one post. How do you give genuine value without expectation and also get leads? I have a golden rule that helps me find the balance.

"Ensure every post provides value, regardless of whether someone responds to my CTA."

You can achieve this goal by using the TASK method.

T = Total value in every post.

A = Add value in the caption.

S = Switch to the Pitch.

K = Keywords to take action.

Total Value in Every Post:

This is where you use your skills as a coach and educator. Teach people something, but don't make it complicated. Remember, you're not trying to solve every problem in one video.

Give, give, give. Give your best tips, insights, strategies, and solutions. Don't worry about giving away too much. Someone has given away everything you know for free already. Make your ideal customer the focus of your post, and have the aim of helping them get closer to their goals.

Remove any lead magnet CTA from the video. Asking for something takes away from the value-driven nature of the post. The video should provide value, regardless of whether the viewer reads the caption. You can direct them towards the caption in the video, but don't blurt out, *"Watch my free webinar."* Most of your audience will hate the thinly-veiled sales pitch.

Add Value in the Caption:

Use the caption to provide more context, information, and insight. Put whatever you couldn't fit into the video in the accompanying text. Apply all the core principles you learned earlier to make your caption easy to read. The goal is simple. Get people from the first sentence to the last.

Switch to the Pitch:

It's not always easy to find a link between the topic of your post and the lead magnet you're promoting. But trust me; it's there. If you find a seamless way to segue to the lead magnet, you'll boost your chances of people taking action.

The CTA needs to feel like the next logical step for the viewer. Your segue and offer need to feel like, *"If you need more help with this, here's where you can find out more."* Don't make it as lame as that, but bring the sentiment to your transition.

In the past, I held back on promoting lead magnets unless it felt "right." I shied away from pitching if the post's topic didn't lend itself to an offer. It made sense, but it hampered my ability to get consistent leads. I started thinking about ways to improve the segues in my captions. I wanted transitions to feel natural, smooth, logical, and effortless. Most importantly, I wanted the reader to find value in the caption. I didn't want them to feel like they were reading a 2,000-character set-up for a sale. My solution? Chris Orzechowski's Super Smooth Email Transition course.

I won't give away everything Chris teaches in the course. We're friends, but he's bigger than me, and I don't want to land in hot legal waters. I prefer to avoid that headache. But, I will reveal the exercise he teaches at the beginning. Here's what you'll need for the task: A pen, a piece of paper, and a timer.

Remove all distractions, and give this your complete focus. Draw three circles on the piece of paper. In the left circle, write "TV." In the right circle, write "Laptop." Set the timer for 60 seconds and write anything connecting these two objects. For example, screen, internet, electricity,

Netflix, sound, images, and connectivity. These words become the inspiration for your segues.

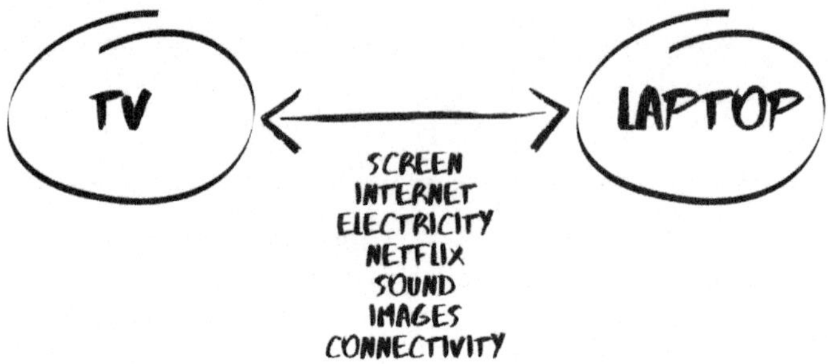

Once you complete the exercise for TVs and laptops, progress to more abstract objects. Look around the room, and pick two random objects. Set the timer, and find ways to connect the two. Seeing links between unconnected things makes the transitions in your captions second nature. Here's a real-world example.

Right now, it's January 2023. I'm in a swanky coffee shop in Paris. To my right, a Barista is crafting a Chemex coffee with precision. (Yes, I am a coffee snob). She pays meticulous attention to grinding the beans to the perfect coarseness. After weighing the coffee to the gram, she pours the water over the grounds. She does so with the utmost concentration. Now for the segue to a social media lesson...

It's like writing a social media strategy. The minor details matter. What others consider a simple part of the process is something I'll take time to get right. Precision and care make for a better coffee. Precision and care make for a better social media strategy.

See how it works? You can segue anything with a bit of practice.

Weight Loss & Business:

- Simple principles that are hard to do.
- The need for patience and consistency.
- Expert help is invaluable.
- Misinformation and lousy coaching are rife.

Copywriting & Making Dinner:

- You need basic skills.
- Following a framework or recipe makes things simple.
- The better the ingredients (words), the better the outcome.

The segue principle extends beyond physical objects and situations. You can also segue from emotions and feelings.

Think about the headache of trying to get leads from social media. Before you read this book, I imagine it was a frustrating, soul-destroying process. Anytime I experience frustration, I can make a simple connection to the same emotion you feel.

The trick is knowing your niche inside-out. When you know their typical thoughts, feelings, and emotions, segues are a cinch. With time, transitions will flow smoother than the perfect pour-over coffee.

People also struggle with the specific words of the segue. But not you...

Use the 16 segue starters on the next page in your emails and captions for a seamless switch to the pitch.

"But what if..."

"Why am I telling you this?"

"Nevertheless..."

"Anyway, here's the deal..."

"Here's the thing..."

"Think about it like this..."

"My point?"

"The best part?"

"What does this have to do with..."

"Listen..."

"Imagine..."

"It's like..."

"You might think that this has nothing to do with..."

"I could go on, but let me get to the point."

"It all starts with..."

"The point is..."

Don't make the mistake of writing a pitch for your lead magnet that's one or two sentences. Sell your lead magnet like it's your paid service.

Get prospects excited about grabbing the freebie. Tell them about what they'll get, its benefits, and why they should get it today. Many of my CTAs are 50% of the caption. Never assume your audience wants what you're giving away because it's free. You still need to sell it.

Keywords to Take Action:

The final element of the TASK Method is the easiest, but it's the part many people overlook. Keywords are one of the crucial elements of the Posts to Profits process that makes it unique.

Keywords make it easy for your prospect to take action. Commenting one word gets them access to your lead magnet. There's no need to click a link in your profile or type a URL into Google. The prospect types one word, and you do the rest. This simple process reduces friction to taking action and increases opt-ins. But, it's not the true genius of the strategy.

When I ask creators if they can track which posts generate leads and which don't, they look perplexed. The typical response is, *"Well, I got 7 leads this week, so something must be working."* But knowing which posts generated leads and which didn't is vital. With specific analytics of each post, you can spot trends and make more of the content that gets leads.

All you need to do is ask people to type a keyword in the comments section of the post and then analyse how many responses each post received. This gives you quantifiable data about how many leads each post generated.

You don't have to use a lead-generating CTA on every post. Sometimes, you'll want to start conversations or encourage followers to save and share. But, anytime you're pushing for a lead-generating action, ensure you measure the outcome. Post with purpose, not to tick boxes on a to-do list.

There's another reason keywords are perfect for generating leads on social media: follow-up. A traditional social media lead magnet funnel would contain three basic steps.

- Social media post with CTA.
- The prospect clicks the URL and opts in via an online form.
- Follow up with the prospect via automated emails and regular campaigns.

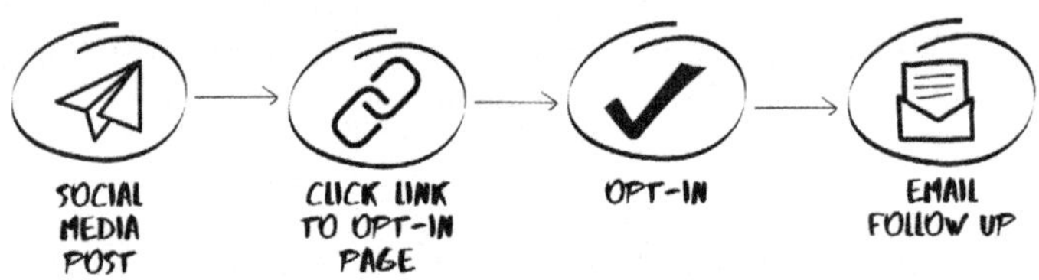

This is fine, but using keywords allows for a more comprehensive follow-up.

- Social media post with CTA
- Prospects comments with the relevant keyword.
- URL sent to the prospect via DMs.
- The prospect clicks the link and opts in via an online form.
- Follow up with the prospect in the DMs and via email.

There are two more steps in the process, but now you can follow up on social media. You can take this process one step further and give opt-ins a massive boost with DM automation.

DM automation is possible on several social media platforms.

"No, Simon. No! Chatbots are so impersonal."

It's true. Chatbots can be annoying and impersonal. But, with the right approach, automation makes everyone's life easier. Imagine the scenario... You've posted on Instagram. You made an informative Reel about calories and included extra tips in the caption. Your CTA told people to comment FATLOSS1 to access your calorie calculator.

When they comment with this keyword, a DM lands in their inbox. They talk with the ChatBot, giving their name and email address to access the calculator. The prospect never leaves Instagram and doesn't go to an opt-in page. There's also no need to wait for you to go online and send the information. The prospect gets what they want, when they want it, on the platform they choose. This customer-centric process boosts your email opt-in conversion to almost 100%. Which approach is more customer friendly? The convoluted "link in bio" hoop-jump, or the seamless automation?

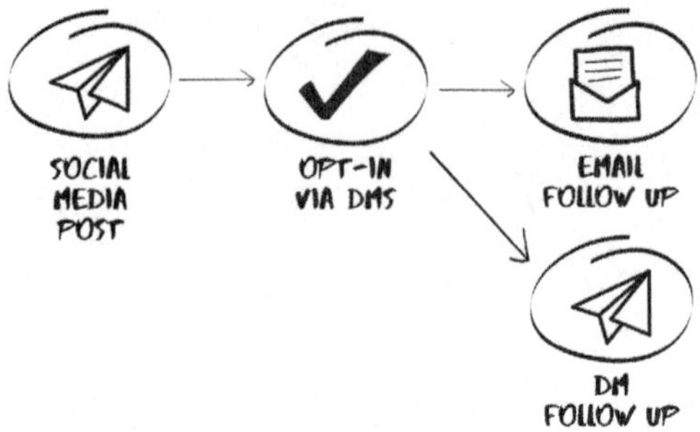

"But, Simon. What about when people want to talk to a human being?"

DM Automation doesn't stop the human conversation. It allows you to skip unnecessary discussions. It gives you more time for meaningful chats with your audience. For example, in my business, DM Automation only triggers when someone uses a keyword. If people to DM me a specific question, there aren't any barriers. I get dozens of daily DMs about courses, coaching, and content. I'm happy to answer them all.

I'll give you another example. One of the pains of selling online courses is sending login details. Customers misplace the email with the login URL or forget their login details. Customers get frustrated when waiting several hours to access their course. With automation, customers can use automated prompts for the information they need. No waiting. No frustration. Automation is only impersonal if you ignore the customer experience.

And think about it like this...

When 100 people DM you asking for the link to your lead magnet, is your canned reply more personal?

Why Good Lead Magnets Fail

Many lead magnets never generate leads. People often make four common mistakes when designing and launching their lead magnets. If you can avoid them, you'll increase your chances of having a successful lead magnet.

1. No Launch Process

Coaches often publish lead magnets out of nowhere. They put a link in their bio and post once without any build-up, expecting the floodgates to open. The response? I've seen more leads in a Dominatrix's sex dungeon. Start the promotion long before launch day to increase your chances of success. You'll find my seven tips for the perfect lead magnet launch at the end of this section.

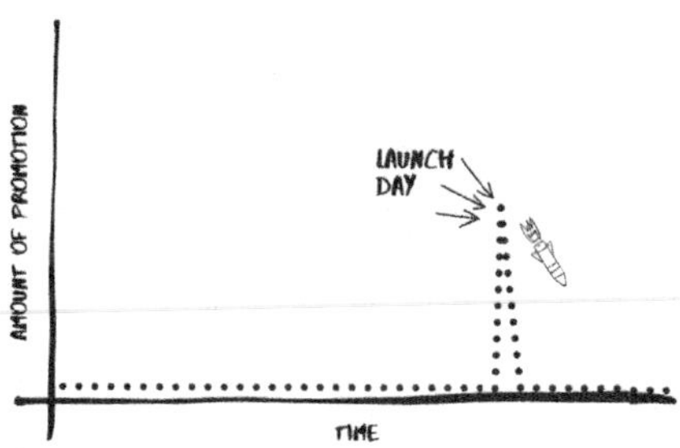

2. The Problem Isn't Immediate

This comes back to understanding your audience and the domino method. Focus on the issue preventing your ideal clients from getting started.

3. Difficult to Access

I've completed hundreds of social media account audits. As a wild, unsubstantiated guess, 25% of those had lead magnets that were impossible to access. Either the links didn't work or led to the wrong lead magnet. If you create a lead magnet, make it easy to access.

4. Design and Delivery is Poor

They say you shouldn't judge a book by its cover, but it's untrue. Make your lead magnet look and feel as professional as possible. If necessary, hire someone to do it for you. It will be worth the investment.

7 tips for the perfect lead magnet launch.

Launching your lead magnet isn't difficult. But, if you want a lead magnet launch that makes investing in your service a slam-dunk no-brainer... which is the entire reason you created the lead magnet in the first place... Then, follow these simple seven steps for the perfect launch. The only time I've experienced a flopped launch is when I deviated from this process. So, pay attention! Your lead magnet is about to go stratospheric.

1. Turn theory into reality.

Hypothesise all you want about your avatar's pain points, but you'll never know you're right unless you ask. Before creating anything, poll your audience. Ask your followers and email subscribers what they struggle with the most.

2. Take them on the journey.

Tell your audience what you'll create based on their feedback. Don't disappear into a cave; only surface when you've finished creating your masterpiece.

3. Go behind the scenes.

Your audience wants to feel a part of the development process. People are more likely to desire the finished product if they feel involved in its creation. If you're creating a webinar, share a sneak peek of the slides and recording process. If you're writing an eBook, show images of the writing process and a few excerpts. Whet their appetite and create anticipation.

4. Set a date.

Tell people when you're going to launch your lead magnet. Whip up excitement and have a countdown to launch day.

5. Offer bonuses.

It could be worth offering a small prize to the early adopters.

The goal is to get people to consume the content and rave about its quality. You can do that by offering a small bonus to everyone who requests access during launch week. You could host a private webinar or throw in a bonus training.

Scarcity and urgency are your friends.

6. Create relevant content.

Create content related to your lead magnet's topic in the weeks leading up to the launch. Tune your audience into your way of thinking. Start attracting people who will love your lead magnet long before you launch it.

7. Launch. Launch. Launch.

It's time to launch. Don't let your hard work go to waste with a half-hearted promotional effort. Talk about your lead magnet whenever the time is right. Go live. Promote it in your stories twice a week (at least), and add it to your carousels as a CTA.

Follow these seven steps to safeguard against a limp lead magnet launch.

What happens after prospects get your lead magnet?

You've published a lead magnet. You're getting leads. Now what? How do you convert those leads into customers? The answer is email and social media nurture.

Following up on social media is straightforward. Message people within 24 hours of accessing your lead magnet to prompt conversation. You can do this with automation, but don't leave everything to the bots. Take over and have a human-to-human conversation when you get a reply.

Email automation is more challenging. Your emails must nurture prospects to a buying decision without your intervention. There are myriad ways to design an automated email nurture sequence. My method is the only way; it's a way.

There are seven emails in the sequence, which follow the four-step FAST structure.

1. Forward the lead magnet.
2. Accelerate the nurturing process.
3. Solve problems with stories.
4. Tackle objections.

FAST email nurture: #1. Forward the lead magnet.

Your prospects came for a lead magnet. It's time to deliver. You can get clever, add some backstory, and hint at what's in the coming emails. But most of all, give people what they came for.

FAST email nurture: #2. Accelerate the nurturing process.

There's nothing wrong with releasing a lead magnet that gets a low score after using the quality formula. It could be the perfect choice to grab prospects' email addresses and start the sales process. But your prospects will be far away from a buying decision. So, your email sequence must do almost all the nurturing. This isn't a problem if you're a copywriting pro. With writing chops sharper than Lorena Bobbitt's kitchen knife, email nurture is easy. But if you're an email novice, you'll need to learn quickly or use a Nurture Accelerator.

There are two types of Nurture Accelerator. The first is the Deliverability Booster. It's vital to get prospects to read your emails. If your emails land in the spam folder, you'll struggle to convert leads into clients. Using a reputable email autoresponder is the first step. The second is to send an email that generates replies. Responses to your emails signal to service providers that they aren't spam.

I use one of two Deliverability Boosters in my email sequences. The first is a simple conversation starter.

"If I could solve your biggest problem with [desired goal] for free, what would it be? Hit reply and let me know. I'll see if I can help."

Not only does this generate replies that boost deliverability, but it starts conversations.

The second Deliverability Booster is the tease of another freebie. This idea comes from the awesome Daniel Throssell (Australia's No.1 copywriter, I hear).

"...Reply to this email in the next 24 hours and tell me the number one struggle you'd love to solve. If you do, I'll send you an extra gift... [Tell them what the gift is]. I don't share this anywhere else. I save it for the select few who reply to this email."

The beauty of this email is you can start conversations with prospects that could lead to sales calls. And the gift could be your next Nurture Accelerator: The Value Shifter.

One purpose of your email sequence is to get people to come around to your way of thinking. You become a go-to person when prospects believe in your methods and share your values. A short pre-recorded webinar is a great way to achieve this value shift. Aim to make the video no longer than 15 minutes. Structure the webinar around the 3 to 5 most common mistakes your ideal clients make. Link the solutions back to specific aspects of your unique mechanism. Use client case studies to show how your method helped them overcome their issues. Include a strong CTA and Boom! You've accelerated the nurturing process within a couple of emails.

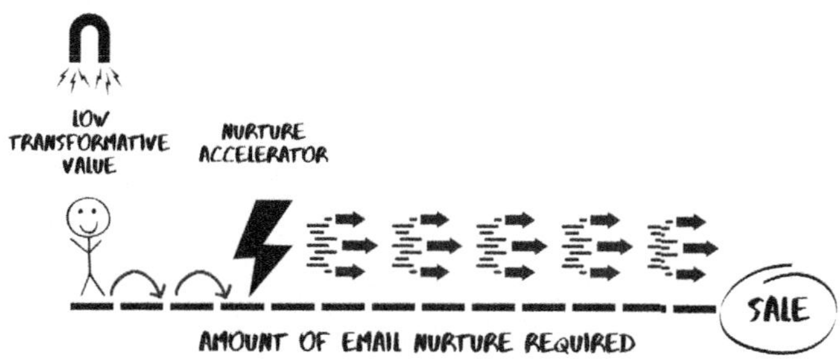

FAST email nurture: #3. Solve problems with stories.

You won't charm everyone with Nurture Accelerators and Value Shifters. Some prospects will need good old-fashioned emails. Address three significant issues from The Problem Path in the third, fourth, and fifth emails. Use client or personal stories to show how you solved these universal problems.

FAST email nurture: #4. Tackle objections.

The last two emails of the sequence should attempt to overcome objections. Think about why prospects are reluctant to book a sales call (it could be that you refer to it as a sales call, FYI). Consider the doubts potential buyers have about investing in your course or service. Remember, you're not trying to convince everyone to buy. Concentrate on the 10% on the verge of a decision.

Whichever way you decide to set up your email sequence, keep your emails entertaining. You won't nurture prospects off square one with dull, boring, self-serving emails.

Blow up your profile with bio-optimising NAPALM!

"I love the smell of napalm in the morning. It smells like... leads." Definitely not Lieutenant Colonel Kilgore.

Traditional websites are dead... maybe. Social media is so pervasive that online service businesses don't need complex websites. (Well, most don't). Sales pages, yes. Opt-in pages, yes. Multi-page websites that cost thousands to build and maintain? Not anymore. Of course, if you want one and can afford one, go for it. It'll be a small way of adding to your brand. But make no mistake. A sexy home page won't rescue a failing business.

No social media platform is the same, but they all have one common element—the profile. The profile is your chance to tell the world who you are, what you do, and why they should buy from you. It's your website. The trouble is most people don't realise the lead-generating power of their profiles. Instead, businesses litter their profiles with junk. If it's isn't highlights of boozy Magaluf vacations, it's endless puppy pictures. Don't get me wrong. I love a puppy picture. But you'll never see one front and centre on my social media profiles. Call me crazy. Call me out of touch. But you wouldn't dream of making photos from drunken nights on the town the focal point of your website. So don't follow the clueless. Don't try to sell your services using inane, cringeworthy content. If you wouldn't put it on your website, don't put it on your social media profile.

I can't give you specific advice about how to set up your profile on every social media platform. Instagram is different from Facebook. Facebook is different from LinkedIn and so on. Also, platforms change so fast that my advice will be outdated before my words hit the printer. Instead of platform-by-platform specifics, I'll share the universal truths applicable to all platforms.

The username is your URL

Usernames should be simple and memorable. Think of your username as the URL of your website. Before you decide on your username, imagine adding '.com' to the end. How does it look? Would you register this URL and drive traffic to it?

@myawesomebusiness looks and sounds great. Adding .com to the end of the username would make the perfect URL.

@my_awesome_x_business_ is terrible. Avoid special characters where possible. People forget the underscores, dots, and dashes. Worse still, you're driving leads to competitors whose username is similar and simpler.

The other username test I often use is 'The Podcast Test.' Picture yourself on a podcast, talking about your area of expertise. You've delivered sixty minutes of solid-gold insights. The host starts to wrap up the episode and asks, *"Where can people connect with you on social media and find out more?"* Would you rather reply...

"Head to @myawesomebusiness on all platforms." Or...

"Head to @my_awesome_x_business_ on Instagram, or @myawesom e._.business on LinkedIn..."

Lousy usernames are a forgettable, lead-losing eyesore. A point that's even more obvious when you consider how they sound. Reading @my_awesome_x_business_ is one thing. Saying it is a horrific four-teen-syllable car crash almost three times as long as the neat version.

"At, my, underscore, awesome, underscore, ex, underscore, business, underscore."

Sometimes, you will need to be creative. With billions of social media profiles, someone might own your perfect username. This was true when I wanted to register @simonmitchell on Instagram. I could have added special characters or numbers and found a close match. But these options wouldn't pass the .com or podcasts tests. Instead, I opted for a prefix to avoid the dreaded special characters. I registered both @iamsimonmitchell and @therealsimonmitchell on the platform. Problem solved. Here are several prefixes and suffixes to inspire your creativity.

@[your name]coaching

@[your name]fitness

@[your name]

@more[your name]

@the[your name]

@[your name]nutrition

@[your name]copy

@[your name]media

@[your last name]

@[your first name]

@thrivewith[your first name]

@yourlifecoach[your first name]

@resultsby[your first name]

@salescopyby[your first name]

There are dozens of possibilities. Search through social media platforms for usernames that grab your attention. Use the structure of what works to create a unique, simple, and compelling username.

No logos in the profile pic

There are two main types of service businesses: ones fronted by a specific person and companies. Take Maverick Goose Ltd, my company, for example. At the time of writing, I have no desire to grow Maverick Goose into a large business with dozens of employees. I don't want that headache. So, I'm content positioning myself as the face of the company. If I wanted to step back and hire coaches to deliver the service, I would allow the company to take centre stage.

The decision you make dictates your profile picture. When you (or someone else in the business) are the figurehead, your face should be the profile picture. The science backs it up. In 2014, Georgia Tech researchers studied 1.1 million Instagram photos. The researchers found that images of faces were 38% more likely to get a like than photos without faces. Those same photos were also 32% more likely to get a comment[2]. It's not a risky leap of faith to assume the same logic applies to your profile picture.

The logic also works with the "social media is your website" theory. Coaches, copywriters, educators, and course creators, are selling themselves as much as anything else. A well-designed homepage for these services would have a picture of the figurehead. A wide, bright smile does wonders for connecting with your prospects. As the cliche goes, 'People Buy People.' Customers want to see and click with you, not a giant image of your logo. You're not selling burgers at McDonald's. You're selling premium services. And people want reassurance they are investing in the right person. Unless no other option makes sense, don't put logos in your profile picture.

First content impressions matter

I couldn't write a book without squeezing in a tale about my online dating history. These stories (of which there are many) have become folklore in my friend circle. My wife loves hearing about my plight so much she forces me to tell these tales at every opportunity. This one is about first impressions. It's about the girl who never left Peterborough.

To tell this story, I need to take you back to 2010. I had been out of the dating scene for seven years and was living a life chained to my career. Meeting new people was hard. So I decided to dip my toe in the online dating waters. Back then, there was no Tinder or Bumble. My site of choice was Plenty Of Fish. As I began flicking through profiles, one girl grabbed my attention. I'll call her Stephanie to protect the innocent. Stephanie was smouldering—sexy. I slid into her DMs faster than milk goes through the lactose intolerant. A couple of days of messaging ensued before we decided to meet. Being the gentleman I am, I offered to travel to where she lived. She picked a pub in Peterborough. I'd never been to Peterborough but was up for the adventure.

Anyone who knows me will tell you I hate being late. So, as usual, I rocked up to the pub well ahead of time. I was dressed smart but casual (I didn't want to look like I made too much effort, know what I mean?). I clocked the perfect table in the corner. I could put my back against the wall, preventing Steph from catching me off guard. Fifteen minutes later, someone approached the table and whispered,

"Excuse me... Is your name Simon?"

I looked up with a face of horror. This wasn't Stephanie. This was... someone. I have no idea who, though. What now? What's the online dating protocol when you need Trading Standards on speed dial? Do you call her out? Do you carry on with the date, then disappear off the face of the Earth? Or do you make some lame excuse and exit fast? I needed time. I went to the bar to get Steph a drink, stopping at the gents to call my housemate. She was a woman of the world—a font of sound advice.

"I'll call in 20 minutes and say that your dog died," was the summation of her genius.

"Seriously? That's all you got?" I said, stunned at the unimaginative response.

With no alternative, we proceeded with the lacklustre plan. But I still had twenty minutes to kill. And what a twenty minutes it was—the weirdest of my life. If you Googled "bad first impressions," this would be top of the rankings. I learned four "facts" about Stephanie that night (although I doubt their accuracy).

Number one. She got married at sixteen and stayed with her husband for ten years. I'm no Perry Mason, but marrying a 16-year-old is illegal.

Number two. Her ex-husband is ten years older than her. Again, I'm not one to judge, but a 26-year-old man marrying a 16-year-old girl is wrong on several levels.

Number three. She didn't own a passport. I suppose this isn't too weird. Many folks don't like travelling, but this fact becomes bizarre when I tell you the next fact.

Number four. Steph never left Peterborough. This "fact" warranted extra quizzing.

"Excuse me? You've never left Peterborough?" I said in astonishment, thinking I had misheard.

"Yeah. Peterborough's got everything I need," she said, with an unflinching straight face. *"I've never gone anywhere else."* To her, it was the most normal thing in the world.

"Wow! Not even to go shopping or for a drive? Aren't you curious?" At this stage, Steph had me hooked. Forget the lifeline phone call. I want to know how this story ends.

"No. Me and my husband loved Peterborough..."

"Where did you go on your Honeymoon?" I interrupted.

Her reply?

"A hotel in Peterborough."

Lord have mercy. I'm done. I thought it was a prank and half expected her to laugh and point out the hidden cameras. But the punchline never came. The call from my housemate couldn't come soon enough. I made my excuses and bolted. See you later, Steph; I'm making a run for it beyond the town border where you can't get me.

It's fair to say that Steph left a lasting first impression on me. A bad impression but a lasting one nonetheless. The moral of the story is that everything you say matters. Whether you're online dating or building an online business, impressions count.

Most social media platforms allow you to showcase specific posts. You might be able to highlight an article or pin a post to the top of your profile. If this function is available, use it. Create specific content that acts as the navigation menu on a traditional website. Don't highlight random posts or even what generated the most likes. Make a solid first impression and start the lead generation process. Draw attention to content that gives people the answers to the following questions.

- Who are you, and why should I trust you?
- Whom do you help?
- What problem(s) do you help these people overcome?
- What specific results will you help people achieve?
- How is your service different from anything else I've seen?
- Have you got proof it works?
- How does your service work?

- Why should I enquire today?
- How can I get started?

Most platforms have a low character limit. So, you might be unable to answer all these questions in your bio. However, most sites allow you to highlight several posts. Use the tools and functions of each platform to create the right impression with your audience. The aim is to speed up the nurturing process and take people from visitors to leads as fast as possible.

Ditch the unnecessary fluff, and focus on promoting your business.

Now let's nuke your bio with NAPALM

Writing an attention-grabbing, niche-specific bio isn't straightforward. Hands down, it's the one thing I get the most questions about when people join my courses. After hundreds of profile audits, I've defined six things every bio needs to get more leads. I call it... The NAPALM Checklist. Follow these simple steps, and you'll have all the ingredients for a lead gen explosion.

Niche

Attention

Problem & Promise

Action

Link

Make it searchable.

Niche

When new visitors find your account, they ask, *"Is this account for me? Is it worth following?"* An easy way to get ideal customers to tap the follow button is to clarify your niche in your bio. The classic, almost cliche way to do this is with the sentence starter... *"I help..."* For example, *"I help entrepreneurs get more leads from Instagram."* It's dated—bordering on unimaginative—but it works. Don't get fussy if you're struggling for inspiration. Clear and unimaginative is better than confusing and clever.

Summing up your audience with one or two words might be tricky, depending on the niche. "Online coaches," "struggling dieters," "bored housewives," and "tech-shy entrepreneurs" all fit the framework. If you're struggling to define your niche in one phrase, focus on the primary problem you are solving. For example, ***"People come to me when their sales pages suck. If sales are slow, I'll rewrite everything to create a rush of new customers."*** With intelligent word choices, you can attract anyone faced with the problem you solve.

Attention

There are thousands of businesses, entrepreneurs, and coaches on social media. You're not the only business working in a specific niche. And you'll never stand out if your bio sounds generic, dull, and uninspiring. Several paragraphs ago, I said the phrase, *"I help..."* wasn't *that* terrible, but it is boring. Often you'll see attempts to spice up this generic phrase with meaningless words.

"Unstoppable confidence."

"Level up."

"Next level."

What does "unstoppable confidence" mean? What are these mysterious levels? I hope it's like Mario Bros. I'm searching for the gold star to skip to the next level without facing the end-of-level boss. It's dumb. And it's often used when people haven't done their market research. There's no more obvious way to say, *"I don't know how to describe what I do"* than these limp, meaningless phrases.

There are two ways to avoid profile purgatory. The first is to revisit the Niche Dump you (should have) completed earlier. Scour what you wrote for unique, bio-worthy ideas and start weaving them into your profile. Second, trawl social media for bios that grab your attention. Go outside your niche and look for bios that tick the NAPALM boxes. For example, you might use an old bio of mine as a template.

"Coaches! Before bad content kills your chances of getting leads, take my FREE Content Health Check. Get a full report & steps to cure your dying IG"

A copywriter helping small businesses write sales pages could turn this into:

"Small businesses! Before bad copy kills your chances of getting leads, get a FREE Copy Audit. Get a full report & steps to boost passive sales"

A fitness trainer helping guys lose weight might say:

"Guys! Before bad diets kill your chances of getting in shape, get a FREE Nutrition Audit. Get a full report & steps to boost fat loss fast"

There are hundreds of well-written, attention-grabbing bios across all social media platforms. Find those that inspire you and start crafting a profile that stands out. But don't start with the most famous accounts in your niche. These people have no issues grabbing attention. And authority rewrites the rules. Given enough clout, some people could fill their bios with poop emojis and still get leads.

Problem & Promise

"Problem and Promise" pop up several times in the book. It's become one of my favourite marketing phrases. It's a concise way of simplifying the advice, *"Focus on pain points and what you help people achieve."* And I love anything that makes marketing concepts simple.

The problem is obvious. What's the one problem you're an expert at solving? Are you the best social media marketer on Instagram? Are you the guy who helps online businesses get leads even if they have fewer than 1,000 followers and their posts have lousy reach? Well, no, that's me. But you get the idea.

Are you an expert at helping struggling dieters overcome cravings and lose weight without feeling like nutrition rules their life? Are you the copywriter who rescues failing e-commerce businesses with compelling sales pages? Whatever problem you solve, be specific. Your ideal clients align themselves with your business if they need the solution. This is simple niching at its finest.

The Promise alludes to the result you deliver. What can people expect from working with you (or at least following you)?

Can you promise to *"heal their relationship with food?"*

Can you promise to *"help them lose up to 10kg in 90 days?"*

Can you promise to *"beat every control with record-breaking sales copy?"*

Tap into the right problem and offer the right promise, and the right people will smash the follow button.

Action

You might not always be able to fit a Call To Action (CTA) in your bio. It depends on the character limit and platform. But, if you can, push new visitors to action, it's a smart move.

The crucial thing to consider is that most people reading your bio don't know you. After all, no one who's followed you for more than a few weeks checks your bio every week. Ensure your CTA is appropriate for first-time visitors. There aren't many people who respond to a high-ticket offer after one interaction. The most common CTA will be to access a lead magnet. But the mistake people make in promoting their lead magnet is they talk about the thing.

"Grab my ebook."

"Access my video series."

"Use my calorie calculator."

Or the worst CTA of all... *"Sign up to my mailing list."* Awful. No one wants to be on your crummy email list. No one wants your lousy, self-serving emails cluttering up their inbox.

Switch the CTA from the "thing" to the results. You'll make it obvious to your ideal clients that they can't do without this freebie. *"Click here to calculate your weight loss calories for free"* is a great CTA. It will get far more clicks than *"Use my calorie calculator."*

Using the TASK Method in Your Bio

The TASK Method showed you how to monitor organic traffic and optimise lead generation. The same approach applies to promoting your lead magnet in your bio. You could tell people to click a link on your profile and redirect them to an opt-in page. But not everyone will opt-in, so you lose these potential leads. But when followers message you with a specific keyword, you increase visibility. You can also measure the impact of changes to your bio and make data-driven decisions. If you change your bio and keyword triggers go down, you know the change didn't work. But if the update boosts keyword triggers, you'll know it was a positive change. The calorie calculator CTA might look like the following sentence using this approach. *"DM me MACROS to calculate your weight loss calories for free."*

Link in Bio

Having a clickable link in your bio is wise, even if you don't direct traffic to it in your bio. Most platforms offer this function, so use it. Give your audience options because not everyone uses social media the same way. Use every opportunity to nurture followers to a sale. You can promote lead magnets, services, podcasts, articles, and more. But there are four "Link In Bio" mistakes to avoid.

Too many options to click

Third-party apps allow you to have several buttons within one URL. This will enable you to promote everything you do to your audience. But this creates a problem. Confused people don't buy, nor do they take action. Don't make the mistake of giving people too many options. Instead, opt for a simple path to the logical next step.

Non-congruent links

If you provide several options, ensure the process is smooth. The first option in your link list should relate to the CTA in your bio. For example, if you tell people to grab your free Instagram guide, the button should say...

"Click here for your FREE Instagram guide."

Any opt-in and sales pages should all use similar terminology. People are sceptical of scammers and spammers. Build trust and increase conversion with simple, congruent processes.

Dead links

It's incredible how many people don't check whether their links work. It creates a poor impression for your followers, not to mention the fact you're losing leads. Test the links you use.

Don't do all the hard work only to let yourself down at the last step.

Using third-party apps

Don't use third-party link-list apps. Don't get me wrong, the apps are helpful, but they steal leads from your business. You don't need an entire website, but I'll assume you've registered your business domain. I'll also assume you have software to create simple sales and opt-in pages. Tick these two boxes, and you can create your own link-list page for use on social media. This seems pointless, but there's a sneaky reason to add this to your to-do list. Whenever someone clicks this link on social media, it's a hit on your website. This means your website will start to creep up the Google rankings. Not only that, but most people will click a link that leads to another page on your site. This reduces your bounce rate—the percentage of visitors who view one page and leave. Even though this tactic may have a negligible effect on the amount of leads you generate, it's better than no effect. Plus, it'll save you money.

Make it searchable

Social media platforms want to make money. You know it. I know it. Zuckerberg and Musk aren't sitting around a campfire singing Kum Ba Yah in the Metaverse. The social media moguls are scheming to hook users on their content heroin. The goal? Attention. Attention is the most valuable commodity for social media platforms. It attracts advertisers. After all, who wants to advertise on a dead platform with no active users? Advertising dollars follow the attention.

Users + The Right Content = Attention.

Nothing keeps users glued to their phone screens more than relevant, entertaining content. Most platforms realise the power of connecting users with content they love. So, search optimisation is vital. Algorithms trawl usernames, bios, captions, and hashtags to categorise creators and their content. Think of this like website meta-data. With this in mind, developers invent ways to tap into the human psyche and get users high on their supply. This drip, drip, drip of content keeps doom-scrolling addicts returning. Your profile gives the algorithms a helping hand. It's like a social media drug mule.

Most social media apps have (or will) become search-driven platforms. Algorithms use keywords in profiles and posts to connect users with relevant content. If I type "nail technician" into Facebook, it will give me a list of accounts with those words in the name field. Entrepreneurs who embrace this concept make their accounts more discoverable with specific keywords. I have a simple way of choosing the best words to weave into your profile.

Imagine your ideal client has tried everything to solve their problems. But, before quitting for good, they give it one more shot. At this moment, when your service would be their perfect solution, what do they type into Google?

"Weight loss coach or fat loss coach?"

"Copywriting courses or sales page copywriter?"

"Life coach or mindset coach?"

"Sleep coach or meditation and mindfulness coach?"

Words matter. A profile mirroring its prospects' search terms will connect with more ideal customers. So, blend how you describe yourself with how your audience describes its problems. For example, when I was a health and fitness coach, most people I worked with wanted to lose body fat. But I used the term "weight loss," not "fat loss." Years of fad diets and diet culture left my ideal customers with a scale weight obsession. To my audience, weight loss and fat loss were the same. Instead of ignoring my prospects' vernacular, I embraced it.

Take some of this Bio-optimising napalm, sprinkle it over your bio, and watch your account explode.

Chapter 17

STAGE 6: SELL

The Six-Step Organic Content Strategy

"Selling is a transference of belief over a bridge of trust. Therefore you cannot sell unless you believe. And they will not buy unless they believe YOU."

Alex Hormozi

They're out there. Sales calls. Love them or hate them, they're a necessary part of the sales process for many online businesses. I'm not the world's expert on sales calls. I hate them. I've created specific elements of the Posts to Profits process to avoid them. These days, the only way to get me on a video call is to become a client. So I'll leave the sales call advice to someone else (Alex Hormozi is a good place to start). But I know something about using social media conversations to get potential clients on calls. And, good news! I've developed a way of doing it that boosts conversions. Better yet, you might be able to do away with sales calls altogether.

Several months before the launch date of this book, I showed an early draft to a friend. I wanted to ensure I was on the right track and my ideas were logical. I didn't know before I started, but writing a book is lonely. You're stuck in your own thoughts for hours every day. Days pass as you tinker with sentences that take less than five minutes to read. I didn't want to emerge from my writing bubble with a jumbled mess of ideas. But my mate's feedback made me doubt my entire approach to social media marketing.

"The Selling section is a bit thin." Ooff! Those words felt like a dagger to the gut. *"Shouldn't this be the bulk of the book? After all, people want to make sales."* Ouch! One puncture wound wasn't enough. He went in for the second and third. And he wasn't finished. *"It's like you ran out of ideas."*

When I asked for brutal, honest feedback, I meant, *"Tell me it's great, and not a single word needs changing."* I knew my friend's feedback came with good intentions, so I sat and contemplated his words rather than jumping on the defensive. I questioned whether I had rushed the book. I doubted whether the barren pages resulted from not knowing enough about sales. After all, I admit to not being an authority on sales calls. But, then, the penny dropped.

Logically, the book decreases in content as the chapters flick by. The Gravity Method lays the foundations of your entire marketing strategy. When you spend time establishing the right base, everything starts falling into place. It's like running a successful business project.

In 2017, I led a team implementing a global online booking system for my previous employer. (It's a boring subject, but stick with me). Years of experience taught me that successful projects start with detailed planning. Projects go off track and spiral out of control without structure. On launch day, the team is pulling pizza-fuelled all-nighters to correct myriad errors. We took our time with the Online Booking project. We spoke with end users to get their feedback. We assessed vendors, developed marketing material, and tested everything. Were there issues? Yes. No project runs without a hitch, but there was no mad panic or all-nighters. The upfront work reduced the pressure at the tail-end of the process.

It's the same with social media sales. The more you define your niche, offer, and strategy, the more sales come to you. When you post the right content and make compelling offers, pre-sold leads land in your inbox. The sales process isn't as intense because you've almost sold the prospect on your service. In reality, you don't need pushy sales tactics.

Something is going wrong if you have to twist arms and convince people to buy.

Now that I've padded out the chapter more with that story let's return to the sales talk. I hope my mate's happier now.

First, a couple of caveats. These techniques will evolve as social media users become savvier to marketing communications. Also, all audiences are different, and all brands are different. You may need to use alternative wording to communicate with your audience in a way that feels more like "you." Don't be afraid to experiment. The following approach is a guide, not a rigid set of rules you must follow or else. Let's begin with the idea of Permission Marketing.

No one opens Instagram with joyful anticipation of what ads will appear in their stories. Users thumb through their feeds for entertainment, education, and escape. So, ramming your marketing message into their face at every opportunity is a lousy idea. It's ignorant of the entire premise of social media. You're ignoring the wants and needs of your audience and putting selfish gain first. And you don't need me to tell you that that's a terrible way to do business.

Instead, marketing with permission puts your audience in control. You let prospects reach out to you when they're ready to learn more about your products and services. If they are the ones to make the first move, it sends a strong signal to you that they need help. Now, you're in a position of power (in a nice way).

The simplest way to use permission marketing is to use keyword prompts. We covered this in the last chapter (remember the TASK Method?). So far, I've only mentioned promoting lead magnets within CTAs. But there's nothing wrong with jumping straight to the sale. I know. I know. This contradicts what I said earlier about not selling on social media. But you can break the rules once or twice a week if you follow the TASK Method.

When potential clients respond to your direct CTA, they give you permission to pitch. But you still have work to do, and this is where our five-step DM framework begins.

The Diagnosis

Resist the urge to start selling immediately. If you do, you're liable to scare the prospect away by appearing desperate and eager. Instead, start by opening up a conversation and getting to the root of the person's issues.

"Hey, [insert first name]. Thanks for the message. Could you tell me your biggest struggle with [desired goal]? It'll help me understand what service is best for you."

(This is a generic, somewhat dull template. Add your unique voice and style to the message. Don't copy it word-for-word. You'll lose sales).

This message gets the potential client to open up about their specific challenges. It puts them at ease by telling them you will offer them the service you think is best for their unique situation.

The Mirroring Statement

If the prospect replies, they'll give you a list of challenges and frustrations. Use your second message to summarise and playback what they said. The crucial nuance is that your next reply must be a statement, not a question. Below is a verbatim message exchange with one of my clients to show you how it works.

Prospect: *Thanks for your response, Simon. My biggest challenge is converting the engagement I get into paying clients. Some of what I do gets high engagement, and some things don't. It's a bit hit-and-miss.*

Me: *Got it. You want more consistency and reliable processes to convert leads.*

Prospect: *Yep, that's spot on.*

The potential client gave me details of their biggest challenges. All I did was summarise what they said in a statement.

Asking another question at this stage wouldn't elicit the same positive response. Often, a question gets a simple "Yes" rather than evoking a *"this person gets me"* feeling. It's subtle but has a significant impact on conversions.

Exploration

After the mirroring statement, move to the exploration phase. The prospect told you their biggest challenges in question one, so dig deeper. Find out if they're doing anything to overcome those challenges.

"Awesome. Do you have a specific approach to try and [desired goal]?"

If they have a plan, ask them how well it's working. If they don't have a plan, ask about their next steps. The chat could move in various directions. Giving you a generic script to apply to all conversations will turn you into a robot. And until AI gets better, robots won't make sales. But there are a few principles I'd urge you to follow.

Listen

Pay attention, and interact with genuine interest. Some people find being human a mind-boggling challenge, but I encourage you to try it. Read what people say in their messages. React and respond as if you're having an in-person conversation.

Imagine you're discussing a person's issues at a coffee shop. They seem tense and nervous about opening up. Revealing their struggles to a complete stranger feels odd. But they pluck up the courage...

"It's been tough. Since the divorce, I've hit a low point." The potential client gets emotional as they utter each word. The prospect leans forward and sips their coffee to steady their nerves. They're finding it hard to say the last sentence—the sentence that reveals the actual cause of their pain. *"I can't find the motivation to take care of my health. I feel worthless."*

"Shall I tell you how the coaching programme works?" You reply. Your words contain the empathy of a rock at the bottom of the Mariana Trench.

Think conversation, not conversion. The conversation isn't about you. It's about the other person and how you can help them. So take a breath, put your revenue goals aside, and be human. It will bring you far more sales than desperate attempts to push for a sale.

Gaps

Find out what they have tried in the past. Why didn't those things work? What are they doing to ensure the same issues don't reappear? How long have they been trying to achieve their goal? You don't need to ask all these questions. Be selective based on the chat. Aim to clearly understand where they're at, their goal, and why they can't bridge the gap alone. It's like mapping out the Problem Path with a real person, not a theoretical avatar.

The next part of the exploration phase is crucial. You must highlight the Realisation Gap. The prospect might believe they're so close to achieving their goal. But they could be delusional. Based on your experience, you might consider them closer to square one than their dream outcome. It's your job to help the person realise how far they are from their goal and how likely they are to achieve it alone. But! You can't do it by telling them. You need to make them realise it for themselves. This way, the prospect bridges the gap to the sale, not you. Investing in your service is now their idea, not one forced upon them.

Asking the right questions at this stage is a make-or-break for DM conversions. It'll take practice. Don't feel disheartened if every conversation doesn't turn into a sales call. Remember, neediness is a killer of conversions. Maintain the position of authority throughout.

Sense?

You want your potential client to see the logic and benefit of what you're saying. So, check in with them throughout the conversation. One of my favourite phrases is, *"Make sense so far?"* Lots of affirmative responses from the prospect bode well when you prepare to pitch.

Permission to Pitch

You've done the hard work; now it's time to ask permission to pitch. Here's how to do it.

"Would you be open to hearing how I can help you [challenges they mentioned at the beginning] and [desired goal]?"

Again, use words and phrases that feel natural to you. Don't copy the stock template. *"Would you be open..."* is a great way to approach your pitch. It's unlikely the person won't hear what you have to say if you've done the exploration phase correctly. At this stage, you're not asking them to do anything but listen to what you have to say. Again, this is a micro-commitment, leading the prospect towards a positive reply to the final question.

The Ask

After getting permission to pitch comes the most crucial message of the conversation. Now, you must decide whether to pitch in the DMs or invite someone to a sales call. There's no right or wrong. It depends on your ability to convert. You also need to balance the cost of your time and the price of the product or service. For example, don't line up sales calls to sell a £49 eBook. But, if you're selling a 90-day coaching programme worth £2k, a sales call is likely the best option.

To invite people to a sales call, use a message with this basic structure.

"Great. If you're open to it, I'd be happy to set up a call to go into more detail about your struggles and how I could help.

I have a 1:1 coaching programme that helps [insert demographic] achieve [insert goal]. It's helped [insert number] people like you [overcome a challenge and achieve a goal].

Are you open to that?"

Again, framing this as *"If you're open to..."* is much more disarming and likely to yield a positive response. Once the prospect says yes, send a link to book a call.

You need a different approach if you're selling in the DMs with no sales calls. Here are my five steps for pitching like a pro in the DMs.

5 Steps to Pitch Like a Pro in Instagram DMs

Message 1: Introduce the solution and link it to the potential customer's challenges.

"Great... I created my online community to help online businesses like yours get consistent leads from social media.

You'll get access to training courses, monthly content, and group coaching calls. I'll help map out your strategy and give unlimited critiques to improve your content."

Message 2: Establish authority and reaffirm that the solution helps solve specific problems.

"As an ex-online coach with a decade of marketing experience, I focus on helping you stand out. Plus, I'll help you implement my Posts to Profits processes to generate consistent leads."

Message 3: Ask if the solution sounds like a good fit.

"Does that sound like it would help you achieve your goals?"

Message 4: Pre-frame the price.

After they've replied, ask what they're willing to invest.

"I'll be honest; coaching isn't cheap. What's the most you were looking to invest in coaching each month?"

Most people will give you an amount lower than what they're willing to pay. So, don't take the first reply as gospel.

Message 5: Do you go higher or lower?

The next message depends on whether the number given is higher or lower than the price of the programme. If the number is higher than the cost of the programme, reply:

"Ok. Great. The programme is £99/month, so it's £50 under your budget. Plus, joining now is risk-free. You won't pay a penny if you're un-

happy within the first month. Would you be opposed to moving forward and getting started today?"

If the number is lower than the cost of the programme:

"Ah. Ok. Coaching starts at £99/month. I know it's above your budget. Are you totally opposed to trying to make that work?"

Most people are unlikely to be "totally opposed" to anything you pitch at this point. Depending on your offer, you could give payment options or find ways to meet their budget. It's up to you.

You may need to handle objections at this point. The crucial thing to remember is that the customer needs information to make a decision. Ask them what specific information they need to decide. Help them connect the dots rather than use aggressive sales tactics.

PART FOUR:

BRINGING IT TOGETHER

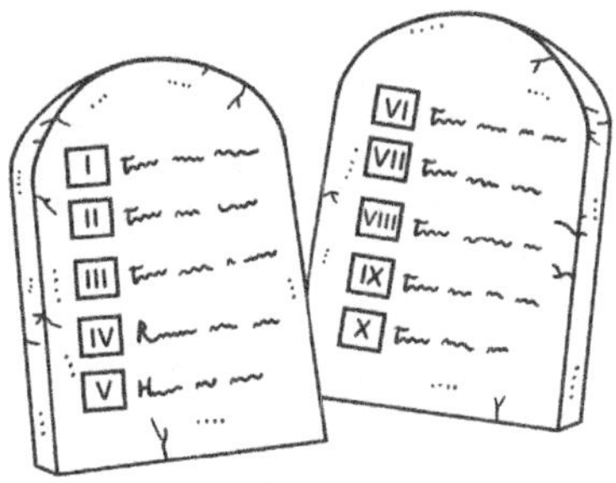

THE 10 SOCIAL MEDIA COMMANDMENTS

CHAPTER 18

THE 10 SOCIAL MEDIA COMMANDMENTS

> And Simon spoke all these words: *"I am the Lord of Leads. Your Content God who brought you out of obscurity, out of the social media abyss..."*

You're holding the blueprint to build a successful online business. But there's danger ahead. Social media is like the Wild West. It's full of Cowboys, Snake Oil Salesmen, and Opinionated Outlaws. They're easy to spot because they follow the same Modus Operandi.

Step One: Read the first chapter of the latest business book (it might even be this one).

Step Two: Post regurgitated, out-of-context summaries to grab attention and make sales.

Step Three: Feel superior, and underdeliver on promises.

It makes them feel (and seem) like they know what they're talking about. Sometimes, it's enough to make you part with your hard-earned money. But from what I see, most social media advice is nothing more than variations of *"It worked for me."* These cookie-cutter marketing tactics are often only applicable in one unique circumstance. Any deviation... Any subtle differences... You're fucked.

Over the past 7 years, I've seen many social media trends come and go. Heck. I've tried them all. Most never worked and did more harm than good. I've created 10 Social Media Commandments based on a similar list by Dan Kennedy for direct response marketing. The 10 rules will help you avoid making the same mistakes I did.

Follow these 10 Rules For Content, and you'll sniff out guru bullshit.

Social Media Commandment #1: Thou Shalt Always Ask For An Action

My opinion on the CTA (Call To Action) has changed. I used to prioritise likes and follows on social media. It felt dirty—the actions of a sleazy salesperson—to mention a paid service. I didn't want to spam my audience with requests to download lead magnets and DM me about coaching. But, my thought process was nothing more than a limiting belief.

In reality, your audience needs to hear about your offer more, not less. If your product or service can help people overcome their challenges, they want to know about it. Your message only becomes spam when what you're offering is irrelevant. Think about using CTAs to progress the relationship with your audience. Post by post, you can inch them closer to becoming a raving fan and customer.

When contemplating what CTA to use, think about these rough guidelines.

1. Use comments and DM action when tracking leads for follow-up on all platforms.

2. Direct people to a URL when you don't care about tracking leads on social media.

3. Add an engagement-based CTA when no other option suits the post.

Favour the actions that nurture prospects toward a sale. After all, if you don't mention your offer, no one else will.

Social Media Commandment #2: Thou Shalt Always Give People A Reason To Respond

If you want engagement, enquiries, and leads, make an offer that's impossible to ignore. This rule applies to anything you sell or give away for free. It even applies to asking for likes and follows (although that might be a waste of a CTA. See Commandment #1). You must stack the offer in favour of your prospects if you want ANY response.

Why should someone follow you? Why should they tap the like button, comment, or share it with friends? Why should someone sign up for your mailing list? Hint... it won't be because of your weekly email newsletter.

Think about how many daily marketing messages the average person receives. I once read that we experience over 400 persuasion attempts every day. Some of the best marketers in the world are orchestrating those persuasion attempts. They have years of experience in grabbing the attention of your ideal customers. If your offer doesn't stand out, don't expect any engagement. The trick is to stop thinking about what you get out of each post. Instead, think about how to best serve your audience. How much can you give without leaving yourself destitute through no income stream? Think back to my "Splinter Offer."

I allowed coaches to access the first module of Social Launch for £5. I gave coaches all the workbooks, Canva templates, and even a bunch of bonuses. The package was worth over £900, and I gave it away for a fiver. My new grand-slam offer increased leads by 700% compared to my previous lead magnet.

The offer and how it's marketed make all the difference.

Ask yourself what you can add to your lead magnet offer to make it more compelling. Define your killer offer and what it would take for someone to do nothing else but respond to your CTA.

Extend this thought process to other CTAs, too. How can you create content so valuable that getting a like and follow is almost inevitable? This is harder than you think. Gifting bonuses is an easy way to stack value. But creating a perfect piece of content isn't always easy.

Make your audience the focal point of everything you do, and they'll reward you with their attention.

Social Media Commandment #3: Thou Shalt Give Clear Instructions

People skim through content faster than ever. You have about half a second to grab attention and get people to consume your content. So, you might think lengthy captions are pointless. But they could be your secret lead-generating weapon.

Well-written captions, packed with keywords, help social media platforms categorise creators' content. Better categorisation means the algorithms show your post to more relevant users. It's SEO for social media. Plus, you can include only so much value in short-form content. The caption allows you to provide more context, information, and value. And here's the important part... Captions allow you to whip up interest in your lead magnet. You can get your audience excited about your offer. The extra words enable you to give people clear steps to get that offer. The trick is to make your caption simple. No complex words where a simple one will do. Appreciate that people don't want to feel like they're reading an essay every time they see one of your posts. When you make it clear what people should do next, they'll often do it. So, use writing software to simplify your writing to Grade 5 or below. This means a six-year-old could understand your post. I'm not saying your audience is full of knuckle-dragging Neanderthals. Nor am I saying that you have to dumb everything down for their deformed Cromagnon brains. The point is you need different writing styles for different platforms. Take this book, for example. Its readability is between Grades 5 and 6. Which is fine for this format. I'm not competing for your attention amidst a melee of social media posts. But, if I were to explain some of these concepts on social media, you'd get the child's book version. I wish it weren't the case, but it's true. People aren't stupid; they're distracted. Keep things straightforward if you want people to take action.

To make the next even simpler for your prospects, use keyword triggers. Use phrases like, *"Comment AUDIT30 below, and I'll send you the details."* This minimises the work your prospects must do to get what they want. They don't have to click a link, figure out which option to choose, and navigate your website. They comment with one word and let you do the rest. If you can use automation, the process is slicker than Gordon Gekko in a mud wrestling contest.

Social Media Commandment #4: Thou Shalt Have A Tracking Method

Question. Would you pay for social media advertising if you couldn't track the return on investment? Would you be happy giving Zuckerberg and Co your cash if you had no idea if it's generating a return? No. You wouldn't contemplate it for a second.

Most people don't have the same thought process for organic content. But your time is worth something. And if your organic content isn't bringing leads, you're haemorrhaging money.

"It's about awareness."

"You need a presence."

"You're brand-building."

It all seems woo-woo to me. It's as if Rhonda Byrne turned her hand to marketing and told everyone to manifest leads. Put down the joss sticks, my friend. Adding glitter to your vision board and chanting, *"I am amazing. I get leads"* into the bathroom mirror won't help. You need a way to track the email sign-ups and dollars generated from your content.

The TASK Method removes the guesswork about what content to create. Most of all, it frees you from the hell of worrying about likes and views. Once you use the TASK Method, you see what content gets leads. And more often than not, content that gets likes and views doesn't get leads.

Social Media Commandment #5: Thou Shalt Think Of Followers As Secondary

Followers are great, but you don't need 100,000 for a successful business. Case in point, I've got a friend who has over 100k but struggles to sell $17 products... and still lives with her Mum.

WHO is more important than the HOW MANY. Give me 1,000 followers who are my perfect clients rather than 100,000 who are ambivalent to my every word.

I'm not saying followers and follower growth aren't necessary. But it is secondary to leads and sales. Focus on scaling an offer that brings consistent leads.

Don't build an audience only to have nothing worth selling.

Social Media Commandment #6: Thou Shalt Follow Up On All Platforms

"Fortune is in the follow-up," so the cliche goes. Most people need several nudges to take action. If you're too shy, embarrassed, or awkward to follow up, someone else will. And when they do, they'll steal your prospects in the process. Start conversations in the DMs with prospects who request access to your lead magnet. Use email automation and regular campaigns to nurture subscribers to a sale. Don't expect a flood of sales from an occasional post and no follow-up.

Social Media Commandment #7: Thou Shalt Create Content That Stands Out

Bland, boring content won't cut it. You don't have to leap about like a court jester on acid, but a little character wouldn't go amiss. I started my online community, Social Mavericks, in August 2021. Since then, I've completed hundreds of profile audits. One of the most common issues I see is content that doesn't appeal to any niche. Use the Last 9 Test to gauge the quality of your content. Ask yourself...

"If I had no previous knowledge of this profile, could I tell who this person helps and what they help them achieve?"

If the answer is no. Your content is (somewhat) generic. If you tell people that you work with a specific niche, show them in your content. Dig into their unique problems. Turn generic concepts into meaningful messages that solve particular problems.

Social Media Commandment #8: Thou Shalt Believe That Your Business Is NOT Unique.

You might work in a small niche with people who have specific demands and expectations. But your business is still not unique. Your goals are the same as every other online business. More leads. More booked calls. More sales. More subscriptions. More members. And the way you'll get those goals is also the same.

Proven marketing principles have worked for over 100 years. Your business is not an exception that defies human psychology. Your content isn't generating leads for one simple reason. You haven't applied the correct marketing principles for long enough.

Social Media Commandment #9: Thou Shalt Believe That Nothing Matters But The Metrics

You'll hear many opinions about the best strategy for getting leads from social media. Business coaches will tell you what worked for them and urge you to follow suit. But in most cases, these "strategies" are nothing more than worthless opinions. It's the plague of marketing in the social media world.

There's an obsession with a new set of metrics. The modern social currency is engagement—likes, views, reach, and followers. But last time I checked, engagement doesn't pay the bills. Call me cynical, but Zuckerberg and Co seem to fuel the craze for these modern metrics. The more people crave likes and followers, the more they're glued to their phone screens. You can almost hear Zuckerberg rejoice! But only ONE metric matters for your online business: sales.

You can have all the followers you want, but you don't have a business without sales. You can have 100,000 views on every video, but you haven't got a business if you can't turn attention into cash in the bank. Yet social media marketers perpetuate their myths. Each of them claims that what they do well is the secret to overwhelming riches. The person with 100k followers says a huge following is the key to success. The person who gets 50k views on every video lauds the benefits of more views. The person whose carousels get massive reach urges you to stop making videos. But marketing is multi-faceted. It's a complex web of strategies, systems, processes, and human psychology. Reducing marketing to a singular desire for more followers, views, or reach is banal. It's like saying that keto is the only way to lose weight. Or that seed oils are killing you. It's tribal marketing. And the tribes are wrong. These people are picking their camp and setting up permanent residence.

Let me repeat. The only metrics that matter (above all else) are leads and sales. Everything else is either irrelevant or secondary. If your content isn't bringing leads and sales, it's not working. Period. But it is working if you are getting leads despite low views and a stagnant following. For example, in December 2022, I gained 294 followers but lost 384. A net loss of 90 followers. If followers were my priority, my content wasn't working. I'd convince myself that I was scaring away potential clients. My reach and engagement were both down in the same period. All the metrics pointed to a content crisis. Time to go back to the drawing board, dream up a new strategy, and try again. But, when I looked at what matters most: leads and sales, the right metrics tell a different story. Leads: up 600%. Sales: up 30%. So my response was to do nothing. In fact, I chose to double down on my current approach. Look at the data and let the numbers guide your decisions.

Social Media Commandment #10: Thou Shalt Embrace Failure

It'll go wrong, and that's ok. Failure is part of the job. The first strategy you dream up will fail. So will the second, the third, the fourth... Marketing is the art of guessing how to make people buy something. What is the difference between good marketing and bad marketing? Better guesses. With time and experience, you learn what works. You're able to refine and hone your message. You use reliable, repeatable processes that deliver value and leads simultaneously. But to get to that point, you need to fail. You must put your best ideas out in the world and watch them die slowly, painfully. In my experience, there's no other option. Sure, courses and coaching can speed up the process and help you avoid making every mistake. But you're not going to transform from shoddy to shit-hot overnight.

Your videos will feel awkward and lame, but that's ok. You'll get more confident on camera and slicker with video editing. Your lead magnets will get zero leads, but that's ok. You'll learn more about your audience, their struggles, and their challenges. And you'll make better lead magnets that pull in leads every day. Your audience won't respond to your CTAs, but that's ok. You'll refine your offer and make it more compelling. You'll write better captions that persuade and convince people to respond.

Think of it this way. You can use shit to grow beautiful roses... if you know what you're doing.

Chapter 19

THIS IS NOT YOUR MOTIVATIONAL SPEECH

> *"Everyone has a purpose in life. Perhaps yours is watching television."*
>
> David Letterman

There's a plague spreading fast. Social media marketing is sick, and it could be terminal. A red X adorns the door—it's marked for death. Greed and deception are rife. And the lies run deeper than you realise.

Bogus claims and wild promises are nothing new. Entrepreneurs seek the shortcut to a freedom lifestyle. Gurus with dubious morals are savvy and pull hard on persuasion triggers.

"Sandra was destitute. She had £100 to her name three months ago." The testimonial reads. *"Now, she's got a six-figure business and living the high life in Marbella."*

It's enough to make the most dedicated entrepreneur doubt whether they have what it takes.

Clickbait headlines taunt. The promise is that this time the miracle is real. After all, it's backed by the latest cutting-edge tactics. It sounds too good to be true, but people want to believe, so they do.

Successful creators reveal the "secret" behind their success. In eagerness and desperation, coaches hang on their every word and whistle their tune. But soon, the reality of the mysterious "secret" becomes clear. It was nothing more than a case of being in the right place at the right time. But who cares? Not the creator who is devoid of integrity. Massive sales of a mediocre course and an overpriced "Mastermind" have them skipping to the bank.

Every few years, a new trend worms its way into the marketing vernacular and burrows into the collective consciousness.

"Email is dead!" The Gurus cry. *"Long live 15-second dancing videos."*

"Show up daily."

"Give value."

Sound bite on top of sound bite on top of sound bite. Hey presto! Marketing fuckery is born.

The problem is status. Society values a large social media following more than genuine knowledge. With the weight of the masses behind them, those with an aesthetic profile turn lies into truth. Like venereal disease spreading through a Magaluf holiday resort, it's unstoppable.

No one wants to hear talk of the boring basics. People want to be bathing in dollar bills by next Tuesday. As a result, entrepreneurs have a twisted view of success. The belief is that hard work and hustle are passé. Mood boards and manifesting will bring you all the riches you desire. And if this doesn't work, you didn't manifest hard enough. Please return to the mood board and douse it with twice as much glitter. It's nonsense. You don't have to work yourself into an early grave. But you will have to do some work (and a lot of it).

Ignorant of reality, people look to social media for more answers. Entrepreneurs hook themselves up to the social media IV, needing a daily fix. Drip, drip, drip come the motivational quotes and vacuous, oversimplified concepts. And despite no progress, people disappear further down the social media shit pipe.

Technology's dominance of modern life has left us thinking there is always an easier way. We can order food delivered to our door without moving off the couch. We can hook up for a no-strings-attached sexy time with a simple swipe. And we can even get express, same-day delivery of a toilet brush (to clear up the marketing bullshit). Modern life has given us an app for everything. Almost. So far, the boffins haven't invented the app to remove all the work from building an online business. But this doesn't stop the would-be entrepreneur from thinking the miracle exists.

The desire for an easy route to success has made finding solutions more complicated. I can't help but think this confusion and complexity is comforting for many people. The fix must be an intricate blend of variables beyond comprehension for mere mortals. It can't be as simple as niche, offer, and content. Can it?

In some cases, great entrepreneurs are to blame. Too many people are afraid to make money. Entrepreneurs often start businesses to help people, so asking for money feels dirty. But this altruistic tendency is no good to anyone. To paraphrase Jay-Z, you can't help the poor if you're one of them. And you can't help your ideal customers if you're broke and living on the bread line.

There are people desperate for help and support. And those people are willing to pay for it. Hell, they've spent thousands on worthless solutions that delivered nothing. So, investing in an honest, relatable person with their best interests at heart is a no-brainer. Yet online businesses are dying faster than ever. They're afraid to say, *"Hey, I've got this great service that I think could help you. Do you want to give me money, and I'll help change your life?"*

Ok, so the pitch could be more subtle. But the idea is sound. Too often, struggling entrepreneurs lack belief.

"...but she's got a six-figure following and all the attention. It's impossible to compete."

Here's the thing. You don't need to compete. You will realise something crucial when you carve out your unique space in your niche. There are enough people who will buy what you're selling and help you build a fantastic life. If you're not where you want to be in business and are too shy to sell, hear this... Pull your head out of your ass and do the world a favour. Sell yo' shit!

"But Simon, I don't know how to get started!"

Well, page one of this book is no better place to begin. Implement what you've read. Grab all the free resources I've compiled at poststoprofi tsbook.com and make a start on the hard work ahead.

Is your business beyond recovery? I don't know. I hope not. But time will tell. Right now, we need to charge the marketing defibrillator and begin resuscitation.

"Clear!"

If you read this book and take no action, nothing will change.

"Charge to 300. Clear!"

You'll drift to the next book, the next mentor, and wonder why you're in the same place in six months.

"Charge to 360. Clear!"

You'll fear failure and never share your talent with the world. And you'll never build the business and life you want.

One thing is for sure. If this book isn't a wake-up call, your business will be in the corner, dying a slow, painful death.

And on that high note... Thank you for reading.

I wish you all the luck in the world.

Stay social, Maverick!

Chapter 20

ACKNOWLEDGEMENTS

> "No one who achieves success does so without acknowledging the help of others. The wise and confident acknowledge this help with gratitude."
>
> Alfred North Whitehead

My business has experienced three moments of significant growth. There are three things common to each moment.

- Financial risk
- Hard work
- A business mentor who cares

Remember the story about my business mentor who sold me his lousy Facebook ad service? Well, I didn't tell you how I dug myself out of that hole.

I thought it was the end. Time to close the doors on Iron Paradise Fitness. Time to head back to the daily drudge of corporate life. But I had one last roll of the dice.

When you get to the brink, you think, *"Fuck it. Might as well go all-in."*

I took what savings I had left and bought four 1:1 calls with Dan Meredith. I couldn't afford them. Heck! Those calls cost almost as much as the Facebook ad investment, even with a generous discount from Dan. But those video calls changed everything.

2020 was my most successful year, despite the craziness of the COVID-19 pandemic. My coaching programme was full. I had a steady stream of leads, all without spending a single penny on ads. I still had stresses and anxieties, but there weren't financial. I wasn't worried about paying the mortgage or putting food on the table.

Dan showed me that I had all the pieces. I just needed someone to help me put it all together. Someone to care. Someone to look deeply into my business and help me plug the gaps. And for this, I am forever grateful.

I'm proud to call Dan a firm friend. He's one of those guys who's there for you, solid as a rock, whenever you need him. He brings a unique blend of "wise craziness" to the world. And I love it. Thanks, Dan, you beautiful mother fucker!

The second moment of significant growth came at the beginning of 2021. A moment of genius from my mentor, Jay Alderton, sparked a complete change in direction. This about-turn would spawn Maverick Goose and change my life.

One of Jay's fellow mentees posted a question in the group forum.

"Does anyone know how to do basic stuff in Canva?" The guy's post read.

Having created thousands of social media posts in Canva, the system was second nature. So, I recorded an impromptu 90-minute tutorial, guiding the guy through the basics.

The off-the-cuff training blew everyone away. Without hesitation, Jay sent me a message.

"Dude. If you can record something like this without planning, you've got skills you need to share." Until then, I hadn't considered myself a design whizz, but Jay saw something I didn't. *"I want you to create a Canva course for PTs. And I want you to launch it in less than 4 weeks."*

(This is a paraphrased version of the chat).

Jay had set the challenge, and I obliged. But neither of us predicted the success of the course. People went nuts for it. I recorded the course using a £9 webcam and a free Loom subscription. But no one cared about the low-budget quality. The course made over £20k in the first couple of weeks. Mind. Blown.

I had always planned to return to my marketing roots. But it was my long-term vision. I was nervous about ditching Iron Paradise Fitness and starting again from scratch. But Jay was bullish about the decision. He kept pushing and pushing for me to focus on Maverick Goose. He saw something I didn't.

Like Dan, Jay is now a firm friend and a guy I trust to provide sound, sage advice. His vision for me and my business gave me the confidence to make the leap. This is what makes a great mentor. Jay cared. But not only that, he fought against my reluctance and insecurity to help me reach my full potential. Without Jay's influence, you wouldn't be reading this book.

This brings me to my third moment of change. I had bought Chris Orzechowski's courses and subscribed to his monthly newsletter. I was a fan.

On March 27th, 2023, Chris's daily email landed in my inbox. The subject title read, "1-on-1 Mentorship." I replied to the email with the eagerness of a kid at Christmas.

I won't lie; the $15k price tag for mentorship made me gulp before hitting the 'Pay Now' button. But within months, I had tripled my Monthly Recurring Revenue. Chris knows his stuff, no question. But it wasn't this massive jump in revenue that I'm most grateful for.

I told Chris I was writing a book. I walked him through the Gravity Method and the TASK Method. His advice was straightforward.

"Write the fucking book, bro!" Since then, he's been on my case to write this fucking book. So, if you've enjoyed these 250+ pages of marketing insights, go and thank Orzy.

Chris's no-nonsense approach was everything I needed to drive the business forward.

These three mentors taught me a valuable lesson, which I hope you learn, too. The formula for business growth is simple.

Right advice + financial risk x hard work = Significant growth

You can't play it safe and reap all the rewards. At some point, you'll need to take a leap of faith.

I couldn't write an acknowledgement without mentioning my fabulous and supportive wife, Maria. She is my biggest supporter and the person who's always in my corner, no matter what. Entrepreneurial life isn't easy. No matter how successful you become, there are ups and downs. There are moments of doubt and times when you feel like jacking it in. Maria helps me keep a level head. She gives me space to work hard and all the love and support I need. Without her, this book—this business—wouldn't exist. I love you, Maria.

I also want to thank my parents, Linda and John Mitchell. When I left the security of my corporate career, they worried. But their support, faith, and love never wavered. I'm a guy who wants to make his parents proud. I hope I've ticked that box, Mum and Dad.

This is like the longest Oscar acceptance speech, but hang in there, I'm almost at the end. My penultimate shout-out goes to my industry friends, clients, and social media followers. I appreciate everything you do to support me and the growth of my business. Everything from liking a post to inviting me to in-person events and podcasts. Your support never goes unnoticed. Thank you.

Last but not least, I want to give a quick shout-out to Team Portugal (you know who you are). Jack said I wouldn't dare mention you in the acknowledgements. Challenge accepted and completed. Thanks for the laughs and putting up with me while I was writing this book instead of sipping cocktails. The next round of Aperol Spritz is on me.

"TP! TP! TP!"

Chapter 21

THE END

> "The part of any book that no one reads."
>
> Simon Mitchell

My aim was to write a book, unlike any other business book you've read. I wanted it to be the most valuable, entertaining, and insightful 300 pages possible. I hope I've succeeded.

Almost every business book ends on a boring note about the author or a plug for their website. But I'm going to end my book with a game. But first, a note about the author (that's me).

I don't know when you'll read this book. And I don't know what courses, products and services I will have available when you do. But I guarantee that if you've enjoyed this book and want to take the next step on the Posts to Profits journey, I will have something for you.

Here are three ways to connect with me.

Exclusive (and free) Post$ to Profit$ resources:

https://www.poststoprofitsbook.com

My website:

https://www.maverickgoose.co

Email:

support@maverickgoose.co

Social Media:

Instagram: @iamsimonmitchell

Facebook: @iamsimonmitchell

LinkedIn: @iamsimonmitchell

Podcast:

Social Mavericks Podcast (available on all major platforms)

Now for that game...

Several chapters contain a hidden literary secret. For fun (and maybe a prize if I'm feeling generous), email me at support@maverickgoose.co if you can guess the secret. You might need to reread the book if you have no idea. But that's not such a bad thing...

Printed in Great Britain
by Amazon

36089914R00175